Everything
I KNOW ABOUT
LOVE
I LEARNED FROM
romance novels

Everything

I KNOW ABOUT

LOVE

I LEARNED FROM

romance
novels

Sarah Wendell

sourcebooks
casablanca

Published by Sourcebooks Casablanca, an imprint of Sourcebooks, Inc.
P.O. Box 4410, Naperville, Illinois 60567-4410
(630) 961-3900
Fax: (630) 961-2168
www.sourcebooks.com

Library of Congress Cataloging-in-Publication Data
Wendell, Sarah.
  Everything I know about love I learned from romance novels / Sarah Wendell.
    p. cm.
  1. Love stories—History and criticism. 2. Love in literature. 3. Man-woman relationships. I. Title.
  PN3448.L67W47 2011
  809.3'85--dc23
                            2011027276

Printed and bound in the United States of America.

VP 10 9 8 7 6 5 4 3 2 1

This book is dedicated to all the fabulous
readers who have come to *Smart Bitches* over
the years to talk romance novels, celebrate
the excellence, and bemoan the bizarre.
You are made of awesome.

And to Adam, who is my romance every day.

Acknowledgments

··············· ♥ ···············

I t is a truth universally acknowledged that I am bad at math. Seriously, howlingly bad. So I can't attempt to add up the number of people to whom I owe thanks because I know beyond any doubt that I will miscount, screw up, and cause all sorts of mathematical mayhem. The fact is, an astonishing number of people were gracious enough to help me with this book, including authors, readers, editors, and mysterious publishing professionals. The communities of romance readers and writers online and off are boisterous and supportive and opinionated and wonderful. So many people from these communities contributed to this book, and I can't begin to say how grateful, honored, and proud I am to have had so much enthusiastic assistance celebrating what the romance community already knows: that romance novels, and the women who read and write them, are amazing.

Thank you for helping me celebrate romance, and what we have collectively learned from it. You rule.

Introduction

One more exuberant gesture and her bosoms would heave themselves over the edge of her gown. Elliott wondered how much more boorish behavior would make it so—and how much of a boor he was to consider enjoying it.

"You're lying," he said in an even tone, trying deliberately to keep his gaze on her face. He wasn't that much of a scoundrel. Well, not entirely.

Alina's eyes narrowed and she took a deep breath, but not deep enough, to Elliott's disappointment.

"I should call you out for that," she said in an equally even tone, but the calmness of her voice was itself a lie. Her cheeks were pink, her hair was askew, and her hands clenched her gown into wrinkles that, should they have appeared on his cravat, would make his valet weep, though in a dignified manner, of course. What could he say next to send her over the edge of reason?

"It won't work," she said.

"What won't work?"

"Your plan." She looked concerned, as if he couldn't remember what they'd just been talking about. How could he follow something so plebeian as a conversation when the most striking woman he knew was one fierce movement away from—he shook himself.

"I think the plan would work admirably," he said, desperately trying to move his brain and its accompanying lascivious thoughts away from any tracts of land south of her chin. There was no reason why his idea wouldn't work. What engaged man wouldn't be tremendously interested in seeing his intended's impending revelations?

"No one would believe you, me, or us."

"Sure they would. I'd make sure of it, and isn't it the standard that the man pursue the woman? My interest in you will be supremely believable." He wouldn't even have to pretend his interest, he realized, and reminded himself again not to look down.

He was so focused on her face that he noticed for a spare fraction of a moment an odd look of sadness. "Why don't you think it would work?"

"Because, dammit," she muttered, and before he could react to her language, she was in his arms, her hands gently framing his cheeks to bring his face to hers, his lips to her own. He found his fingers just beneath the curves he had been trying not to look at, and he was struck to learn he didn't need sight. Touch was much, much better: the warmth of her, the firm but soft bend of her waist, the northward curve of her breast. He'd had no idea how much better this could be than trying not to look.

But despite knowing with all certainty that her décolletage was a precarious thing, he couldn't allow his fingers to tilt the edge of her gown in his favor. This was his intended, after all. His almost intended, anyway, and as his friend and his fiancée, her honor was about to become his responsibility...and how on earth were those her lips moving over his, an embrace and exploration that made him feel as if the top of his head were about to lift off? His hands followed the curve of her side to her back, away from temptation yet bringing it closer. She was firmly pressed against him as he deepened their kiss, touching her with his eyes closed. He really didn't need to see anything. Touch was too much, in fact.

Suddenly she stepped back, though not out of his arms. He held his arms around her as she stared up at him, flushed and breathing a touch too fast.

"I don't see that as a problem at all," he said.

So what do we learn from this scene? That breasts have hypnotic powers more potent than most women realize? No, though they likely do. That men try to behave according to etiquette though that can be a struggle? No, but that's likely true as well. That women can have sexual desire, and act on it, and take risks to grab what they want and plant a big wet one on a gentleman's shocked but willing self? That her desires are as important as his? Yup. Definitely.

If you're a romance fan—and I bet you are—you know that reading romances can teach you a great deal about love, sex, and relationships. In fact, romance reading has probably already taught you more than you realize. You might not be kidnapped by cross-dressing pirates and held for ransom, or find yourself outrunning a serial killer with the help of a very handsome, taciturn detective, but you will always find conflict in your relationships, whether it's bills and debt chasing you down a dark alley, or precarious sexual fulfillment lurking in your bedroom.

But fear not. Inside those stories is everything you need to have a happy, loving relationship. From books like *Seducing a Sinner* and *Rescuing the Rake*, you can learn about tricky subjects like Valuing Your Emotions and Having Real Conversations about Sex.

Welcome to *Everything I Know about Love I Learned from Romance Novels*. In this handy little book, we can celebrate all the wonderful things we've learned about real-life love and romance that are hidden and not-so-hidden inside the average romance novel. What, you thought all those heaving bosom covers with impossibly Technicolor eye shadow were just for visual embarrassment and titillating thrills? Nope. Romance novels are much more complex than meets the eye—and we readers of romance know that better than most.

It's not hard to discount romance, and it's easy to take them way, way less than seriously. After all, there is a 95 percent chance that a romance novel cover will feature a mullet. Enough said.

But romance novels are complex and emotionally driven tales of courtship. And what better way to learn about relationships and how they start, fracture, and become stronger once repaired, than to read about those relationships in many, many permutations and variations? In all the thousands of romances where the boy meets the girl, stuff happens, and they get back together, there are a million-plus possibilities of how to repair what went wrong. And we're going to look at every one, from amnesiac twins and what they can teach us about truthfulness and identity to bank-robbing cowboys and what you can learn from them about bad boys and perhaps avoiding felony charges.

Who am I? And have I robbed a bank? No, not so much. I'm Sarah Wendell, better known as Smart Bitch Sarah from the romance novel website *Smart Bitches, Trashy Books*. *Smart Bitches* reviews and discusses romance novels with a readership of many thousands of readers around the world—there are more romance fans than you dare suspect, and we're all very intelligent, fabulous dancers with minty-fresh breath, and as a bonus, we're all quite savvy when it comes to relationships too. Reading romance, a genre focused on the emotional development and self-actualization of the heroine and hero (a fancy and academic way of saying they get their shit together and grow the hell up like damn), gives romance fans a deep, multifaceted, all-encompassing lesson on how human relationships work. Many of us find ourselves in the role of advisor to our friends as the person others turn to for help with problems.

Ironically, many people who disdain the romance genre and look down on the women who read it presume that reading about courtship, emotional fulfillment, and rather fantastic orgasms leads to an unrealistic expectation of real life. If we romance readers are filling our own heads with romantic fantasies, real men and real life won't and cannot possibly measure up to our fairy-tale expectations, right? Wrong. Wrongity wrong wrong wrong. That accusation implies that we don't know the difference between fantasy and real life, and frankly, it's sexist as well. You don't see adult gamers being accused of an inability to discern when one is a human driving a real car and when one is a yellow dinosaur driving a Mario Kart, but romance readers hear about their unrealistic expectations of men almost constantly.

We're going to put that sorry notion away for good. In this book, you'll hear from me and other romance readers and writers as we explain both what we've learned about ourselves and about relationships. Sometimes the fantastical and impossible, such as the space captain with a streak of honor, or the sinking pirate ship populated with crewmen with impeccable manners and perfect teeth, can help translate reality better than any self-help book ever could. When you see your problems blown up into, dare I say, fantasy proportions, your real problems don't look so insurmountable. Fantasy, instead of distorting reality, can help you comprehend your reality.

For example, in many paranormal romances, especially urban fantasies, the fate of the world, if not the fate of the universe, may hinge on whether or not the heroes of the story figure out their pesky relationship problems and beat the bad guy. Their ability to kick ass and to kiss each other are equally important, because if they don't

> You don't see adult gamers being accused of an inability to discern when one is a human driving a real car and when one is a yellow dinosaur driving a Mario Kart, but romance readers hear about their unrealistic expectations of men almost constantly.

work their shit out, the planet might blow up. Comparing your current difficulty to that level of "OHCRAPNO" might help you gain perspective on how to handle it, and how to stop it from happening again.

This is not to say that problems are not important—they absolutely are. But no one knows better than romance fans that most problems are also very likely fixable with varying applications of hard work and some risks or maybe a righteous smack down with a broadsword and a photon-charged handgun.

Now, before we move on to the kicking of ass and the fixing of things, let me share with you The Rules of This Book. Yes, there are rules. Fear not, for they are easy and friendly rules.

The First Rule: Happiness is serious business, but I do not take many things too seriously. And by "things" I mean pretty much everything. So this is not a book wherein you'll be asked to journal or spend time holding your own hand, envisioning willow trees and flowers with no pollen to make you sneeze as you drift on a tranquil riverbank, reclining in an outlandishly comfortable rowboat with the one you love.

HEY! WAKE UP!

Techniques that bring you to some understanding of yourself are all good—but that is not what this book is about. This book is about celebrating romance novels for every important thing they teach us about ourselves, the people we love, and the relationships we value—and the sex we have. That alone should tell you: expect jokes about man-titty and mighty wangs, and when we get to that chapter about sex, expect the insertion of seriously turgid bad puns.

The Second Rule: Each chapter is defined by a specific lesson we romance fans have learned that is demonstrated by countless romance novels—along with extra content for fun, games, silliness, mayhem, and shenanigans. If you're a romance reader, no matter how old you are or how old your relationship may be, I'm willing to bet a stack of paperbacks that you're already aware of some of these ideas, if not all—even if you didn't realize it. After many, many unwilling dukes and smoldering tycoons meeting their matches among the best and bravest of heroines, we romance readers know what behaviors can help someone enjoy a happy, healthy, meaningful, and satisfying relationship, and which behaviors can screw it all up in a damn hurry.

Many romance readers and writers helped with the creation of this book, and there are quotes from writers you may have heard of, writers who are new to you, and readers who may be just like you—terribly passionate about romances. Some readers I quote by their real names, and others I attribute using their online pseudonyms. Regardless, all of the quotes in this book came from individuals who love romance, and have read metric tons of it.

The Third Rule: Not every situation may match, but the basics of romance, both in real-life and in literature, are simple. Unless your veins are filled, as my friend Billie says, with brimming levels of crazysauce, you are probably a kind person who is entirely capable of loving someone and being loved in return. We get a lot of terrible examples in mainstream media and entertainment on how to treat people we love. Between the murderous glares, misery, mayhem, and acts of momentary weakness played up for maximum laughter, there's a lot of How Not to Treat People. Romance novels are the antithesis of that example, and we readers are fortunate to indulge in stories that are uplifting and hopeful in the end. So if you're harboring some stalwart prejudices about the romance genre, it may be time to rethink them. No, it's definitely time to rethink them. Romances can be a rare but valuable example of how to treat people.

THE RULES OF THIS BOOK

1. Happiness is Serious Business—but don't take me, yourself, or anything else too seriously. Taking yourself too seriously is tiresome. The penalty is mullet.

2. There are specific lessons to be learned from romance novels, as well as mayhem and silliness, too. Mayhem, you may be surprised to learn, is very good for your sex life.

3. The basics of romance, and how to treat people, are surprisingly simple—you just have to rethink any prejudices about the romance genre first. You have to rethink any prejudice, really, including the ones about mullets. They are (allegedly) good for your sex life. So I've heard. Not that I know this personally or anything. ***puts on hat***

So now that we know the Three Rules of This Book, let's get to work. Here's a romance-tested idea that I bet you already knew: the "happy ending" is actually right now. It's not somewhere down the line into the misty future. Everyone deserves a happy-ever-after. Everyone deserves a happy, healthy relationship. Bottom line, everyone deserves happiness, period, full stop. But, as that motivational poster so tritely puts it, happiness is the journey, not the destination. And as Nora Roberts has said many times in interviews, the story of a romance is not the happy ending, but the journey to that happy ending. Thus, every story is different, unique, and ultimately happy.

Romance fans can tell you, happiness is created in the present, not as a wish for the future. The first rule of your happy-ever-after is to be happy right now.

Prepare ye for a moment of touchy-feely-squirminess: that means the first, most-important relationship you have is the one with yourself. If you are happy, content, and capable of taking good care of yourself, whether that's an hour of working out or an hour of reading with a dish of ice cream (and I heartily support both), you're on your way toward happy-ever-after because you care about yourself now. In other (really sickly twee, I admit) words, happiness is the present we give ourselves in the present, and its presence in our lives is a present to the world. (I just totally made you throw up, didn't I? Sorry about that.)

Has anyone told you? You look marvelous today. (When's the last time a book complimented you, and meant it?)

Moreover, happiness is not created by the presence of someone else in your life. Happiness and joy should already be hanging out with you (and complimenting your appearance) when you encounter someone else who captures your attention.

That someone else augments and adds to your happiness— sort of like fantastic icing on a rich, moist cupcake, or a really savory and delicious gravy on your already-gourmet dinner. You are the most important element in the process of finding your happy ending, and you must start with happiness already riding shotgun in your life. A small dose of romance can add to that happy-happy, reminding you that things will all work out, and that, yes, you are marvelous as you are.

But romance isn't merely the printed version of a "There, there" ham-fisted pat on the head. Romance, in addition to being All about the Happy, is also mentally active—and is, we all freely acknowledge, a form of entertainment. Romance is fun! It's sometimes emotionally twisting, or light, sparkling comedy, or straight-up sudsy, fluffy fantasy, but it's fun. But reading romance—and reading in general—is, and always has been, a mentally active pastime.

Compare reading with television viewing: With TV, you passively sit and receive visual and auditory stimulation. With reading, you actively fill your mind and absorb the story mentally while embellishing with your own creativity. The reader creates the voices, imagines the scenery, and envisions the ambiance. Some readers dislike seeing cover models' faces on the book jackets because they want to imagine the faces themselves.

Because of that involvement, women are very critical of their romance-reading entertainment. This is not a surprise for me, since I review and critique romances every day, and the

Smart Bitches, Trashy Books website is largely fueled by the passion of romance readers gathering to talk about what rocked their worlds or what made them irate at the poor quality story. That passionate response (pun intended) is created because romance-reading is complex. It's not a simple endeavor, all that mental creation and emotional connection. The entertainment and creative value is huge—and makes for a very personal and often vivid response in the reader, because if the reader is actively involved in the reading experience, she is giving of herself and wants to be fulfilled. A bad movie might create a feeling of disgust or disappointment, but the same two hours spent with a bad book can create a much stronger negative emotion, up to and including outright rage. Just check out some Amazon book reviews if you don't believe me. Hell, check out some of my D and F reviews on *Smart Bitches, Trashy Books* for evidence of bad-book-rage. It's just as true for the positive response as well: good romances will create an absolute joy and possibly the desire to forcibly beat someone with a paperback until they agree to read that fantastic book you've just finished. (I refuse to incriminate myself by stating whether I've committed such an act.) (Oh, screw it, I totally have. C'mere so I can beat you with my copy of *Bet Me*.)

That incredible positivity at the end of a good romance is part of why romance-reading is so addictive: that emotional lift at the end creates a sustained feeling of happiness, and if readers don't get that expected joy, they are not happy about it, because, oh boy, do they know what they are missing. And when they don't get what they wanted in a book, they are the exact opposite of happy—and that goes for me too.

I've often joked that romance readers have a sound that they make when they finish or even talk about a wonderful book they've read. I can't transcribe it here, but it's somewhere between a sigh and a moan, similar to the sound you make when eating the most delicious meal when you're supremely hungry, or when you finally come into a warm room from a cold day.

The happiness that comes with finishing a good romance also means that this happiness spreads. Reader Liz Talley says that the bonus happily-ever-after (more commonly known as the HEA) "has to give some chemical reaction in the brain that promotes satisfaction and happiness. I can't tell you how many times I've closed a book, sighed, and thought 'Today will be a good day.'"

Romance novels are both the story of the characters finding each other, and the story of finding themselves deserving of the effort that creating a happy-ever-after requires. Happiness might be as difficult to spot as an undercover duke operating a cattle ranch in Texas. But if you're already familiar with joy and contentment, your continued happiness will be as easy to spot as a plucky nineteenth century heroine dressed as a boy. I mean, doesn't every nineteen- or twenty-year-old woman fit into a ten-year-old boy's clothing? Of course they do. I've been to the mall and time-traveled to Regency London. I know these things.

Cross-dressing and tight pants aside, if you want your happy ending, you start with a happy beginning. So let's start right there: you, you holding this book in your hands (hi there!), you're awesome, and because you read romance, you're smarter than the average savvy person. Welcome! Let's celebrate all we've learned and loved in romance novels.

LORETTA CHASE PRETTY MUCH KNOWS EVERYTHING

As I was writing this book, asking every romance novelist I could think of for her perspective and querying readers for their ideas on how romances have affected them personally, I asked one of my very favorite writers for advice. Loretta Chase has written some of the best romance novels ever in the history of the universe, and I say that without exaggeration or hyperbole. Her books are amazing examples of characterization, with strong women and challenging men, and stories that take place all over the world.

When I asked for her perspective on hero and heroine behavior and on character traits that are required for a romance, her response was so illustrative that I had to include it in its entirety.

Dear Sarah:

When I started thinking about rules, I immediately had an avoidance reaction. I hate the idea of imposing rules on the genre, because someone can come along and break them beautifully. But then I thought about my rules for character traits, and I realized most of my answers were in the movie *The Wizard of Oz*.

THE WOMAN IS IMPORTANT

Interestingly, the hero of the movie is a girl. Everything

revolves around Dorothy. Romances are one of the few genres in which the woman really matters. The hero might drive the story, but he's focused completely on the heroine. Oh, yes, he might have to save the world or build a canal or fight murderous antiquities hunters, but those are little problems to be solved on the way to winning She Who Is the Love of His Life. Forever. And with whom he'll have the best sex of his life. Ever.

> **When women read romances, they can live for a few hours in a world that looks like real life but is more delicious.**

Right there we have our obvious fantasy element. All women know this is not the way it is in real life. Among other things—and I have to leave out politics and the media to keep this at a manageable length—in real life men imagine having sex with other women; the hero of a romance barely even sees other women after he's met the heroine. In real life, men compartmentalize; in a romance, most of the compartments are filled with Her. In real life, men are easily distracted by, say, golf or a football game, when their women are trying to tell them something; in a romance, the hero is totally distracted by Her.

CHARACTER TRAITS

The Lion, Scarecrow, and Tin Man are seeking traits that, combined, make my idea of a romance hero—Courage, a Heart, a Brain—and Dorothy, who has all those traits, is a heroine. Equally important, we can relate to all of them at some very basic level.

Seeking to become complete. All the characters are imperfect, but in the course of their journey, they bring out the best in one another. As a team, they become a sum greater than the parts. In a romance, the hero and heroine bring out the best in each other and again, it's more than that: these two people could do all right separately, but when they're together, they create something that transcends who they are as individuals. And I think the great sex we give them—the transcendent sex—is symbolic of that.

Journeying home. Dorothy is trying to get home, and that is my take on finding the Love of Your Life. When the hero and heroine commit to their relationship, it's like a homecoming: one finds one's heart's home in the loved one.

Individuality. Like these movie characters, the hero and heroine of a romance novel—or any genre novel—need to be larger than life. Maybe in a romance novel, the couple's problems don't amount to a hill of beans, as Rick tells Ilsa in *Casablanca*. Maybe they're ordinary folks, like the ones who peopled LaVyrle Spencer's books. But the author makes them big in some way—memorable.

Appeal. I don't think there's a rule that characters need to be beautiful. Most of us have written our *Beauty and the Beast* or *Ugly Duckling* stories. However, I'm shallow, so I make all my heroes tall and hot (at least to the heroine). They don't need to be, but my feeling is, this is a fantasy and we all know it and so why not make the hero fantastic? The heroine doesn't have to be attractive—except to him—but we need to understand what draws him to her.

> "In real life, men compartmentalize; in a romance, most of the compartments are filled with Her. In real life, men are easily distracted by, say, golf or a football game, when their women are trying to tell them something; in a romance, the hero is totally distracted by Her."
>
> —LORETTA CHASE

Faithfulness. Sexual faithfulness isn't an element of *Wizard*, but its friendship counterpart is there, and I think sexual fidelity is crucial to the idealized friendship of a romance hero and heroine. Once they start down the obstacle-strewn path of the relationship, he needs to be sexually faithful. See above re the woman matters.

But faithful applies in other ways: He is or becomes the kind of man a woman can count on. He'll be there through thick and thin. So will she. Again, real life can be so unstable and people are constantly having the rug pulled out from under them. The romance myth offers the beautiful alternative.

IMPOSSIBLE OBSTACLES

The history books are littered with "Truth Is Stranger than Fiction" stories. Couples overcome religious differences, racial differences, political differences. They find a way to make things work, even when they have mutually exclusive goals. That said, it's no good putting in historical fact if the readers won't buy it. The obstacle to be overcome and the way it needs to be overcome must be plausible within the context of the story.

Once the house falls on the witch, we're ready for the rest of the *Wizard of Oz* extravaganza. We, including children, know it isn't real. It's a story! But we know how to suspend disbelief. So we'll believe, for the time of the romance story, whether the impossible obstacle is physical or psychological. In real life, not all that many

> "I would never recommend shooting a man to help him get his head on straight."
>
> —LORETTA CHASE

people overcome deep stupidity about something or mule-headedness or psychosis or neurosis. But part of the myth belonging to romance is this element of healing, with love being the balm. Again, don't we wish that could be true in real life?

THE CHARACTERS LEARN TO HAVE A HEALTHY RELATIONSHIP

My sister tells me that *Lord of Scoundrels* was impressive in that way, but you know, I would never recommend shooting a man to help him get his head on straight. But fantasizing about shooting him might help a woman get through a rough day.

There were a lot of books dealing with unhealthy relationships (can you say *Wuthering Heights*?) that left an impression on me as an adolescent, but the great book about two people learning to have a healthy relationship is, I believe, *Pride and Prejudice*. The change happens by degrees, and it takes time, and Elizabeth and Darcy overcome a social difference that, for the time, was a considerable obstacle. It happens in the context of family and friends—the gossip, the backbiting, the changing opinions, the family tensions, the interference, the competitiveness—it's all there, and it's so human and so well done that teenagers reading the book today can relate. Elizabeth reading Darcy's letter, for instance, and the way her view of him begins to change, is I think one of the great examples of character growth.

I know people are going to say that isn't a romance novel; it's literature. But it's both, and don't we romance authors all wish that might be said of our work some day centuries hence?

Loretta Chase

WHAT ROMANCE ARE YOU?

Ever wondered which romance novel you would be, if you were a romance novel? Of course you have. Who hasn't wondered which paperback subgenre they might be, on a metaphysical or psychological level? Duh.

Anyway, your late-night ponderings are answered with this handy, and somewhat bizarre, chart. Once you've identified which type of romance novel you are, you're only a few hundred thousand books away from knowing the secret to all mysteries, including why paranormal investigators wear four-inch heels and leather pants to work.

	Regency	Western	Harlequin Presents	Contemporary
How do you like your steak?	Well done	Mooing	In a boardroom	Au poivre, cooked by hero
Who is your preferred dictator?	Napoleon	Stalin	Mussolini, the original "Italian Stallion"	Castro
How many pairs of black pants do you own?	0	1	1.75 million	∞
What is your favorite dessert?	Pudding, in a trifle	Biscuits	Angel food cake	Crème brûlée
What is your favorite holiday?	Boxing Day	Independence Day	Boss's Day	National Fruitcake Day (12/27)

Chick Lit	Erotica	Romantic Suspense	Paranormal	Historical
British	Hot, with béchamel cream sauce	Under indictment	Hairy	Medium rare
Lenin	Caligula	Kim Jong Il	Mao	Franco
25	1 (if the pair in a pile on my floor counts?)	5	10. And they're all leather. SQUEAK FREE leather.	Pants?
Fat-free ice cream sandwich	Whipped cream	Anything on fire	Ice cream truck	Melons
May Day	S&BJ Day (3/14)	Winter Solstice	All Saint's Day (duh)	Talk Like a Pirate Day (9/17)

We Know Who We Are, and We Know Our Worth

♥

AKA: SEEING YOURSELF IN A ROMANCE NOVEL IS NOT A BAD THING!

Romance readers take a lot of heat for their love of the genre. It's fluffy pornography, it's fantasy-land, and it gives readers unrealistic expectations of real life—oh no!

That right there is deep-fried hogwash. Romance readers are savvy people who can celebrate the fantastical elements of the genre—what, like every murder gets solved in real life like they do in mystery novels?—while recognizing themselves and familiar situations in each plot. Harlequin CEO Donna Hayes says that romances allow women to see pieces of themselves reflected in the books they read—and she's right. We aren't looking for mirrors of our entire lives, just bits of familiarity—which is why we can learn so much from them. Those pieces of familiarity can be very illuminating.

As a rule, the heroine is usually the focus of a romance, but it's not just all about her. It used to be that the hero would show up at some point and be present in a few key scenes, notably marked as "the hero" by the number of times the heroine would notice him, and how amazingly handsome/smart/dangerous/all-of-the-above he seemed. Nowadays, romance novels, as defined by what's currently popular—and romance is popular, to the tune of over a billion dollars annually, according to the Romance Writers of America—feature the stories of both the hero and the heroine as equally important.

So what does that mean for romance readers? Well, for starters, we read a lot of romance, and we meet a lot of heroes and heroines. We're reading narratives about a woman's self-fulfillment and her own achievement of happiness, whether that's beating the bad guy or finding her way back from a trauma, and we're experiencing the repeated discovery of someone who not only fought for that happiness but realized that she was worth that struggle.

In short, romances teach readers that we should know ourselves, and value ourselves, in order to find happiness. Romance readers experience the repeated discovery of someone who not only fought for her happiness, but realized that she was worth the struggle. That's the first lesson of romance novels, really: romance is found in how we treat ourselves. Would you want to read a three-hundred-page novel about some woman who beat herself up constantly for being those extra few pounds overweight and having the wrong shoes? Maybe, like many of us, she does that every once in awhile, but characters worth reading about eventually conclude that they are awesome as they are, and don't need to put themselves through abusive crap like that every time they get dressed.

Everyone has their kickass outfit, the clothing that fits and flatters and makes the wearer feel invincible and, well, kickass. A romance heroine arrives at that feeling more and more often, particularly if she begins the story feeling poorly about herself, because feeling kickass is the first step to a long day of awesome. Reading that type of self-discovery teaches clearly and openly that women are valuable and awesome.

Romance is found in how we treat ourselves.

So how do romances teach the value of knowing yourself and your worth? Well, just reading one is an act in and of itself that demonstrates that you care about yourself. If you're like me, there's hardly a moment in your day when you're not doing six things simultaneously. If you're reading, then you're likely doing just that one, indulgent thing.

Indulging yourself is a very, very noble task. Don't stop doing that. You're giving yourself a break, an escape, and a moment of relaxation—and if you've noticed the workaholic, wired culture many of us live in, that cessation of constant action is a true respite.

Not only are you indulging yourself, but you're indulging yourself with, literally, happiness. You're reading a reminder that problems work out, challenges become easier, mysteries get solved, and everyone involved can live happily ever after. There is absolute value in reminding yourself that happiness is a worthwhile endeavor.

Harlequin, which publishes over a hundred romances each month, can tell you (and me, actually) a great deal about the value of romance for its readership. Harlequin has an entire corporate division dedicated to researching its customer base, and they host focus groups where they ask readers to explain why romance is valuable to them—and not just Harlequin romance, but romance in general.

Janet Finlay, head of research for Harlequin, says that in each focus group, much to her con-

Reading a romance novel is indulging yourself in happiness.

tinued surprise, there are always women who can remember with great and vivid detail the first romance they ever read. She says that listening to women share details about the first romance they read is much like listening to someone share a story about a truly special moment in her life. Readers can remember details of that first romance, even if it was over thirty years prior.

She's totally right. I have long had a similar theory that romance fans do not ever forget that first romance novel, especially if they enjoyed it. For example, the first romance I read was Catherine Coulter's *Midsummer Magic*. I read it in 1991. I can still remember where I found it (in the public library), how I found it (petty larceny), and who introduced me to romance (a high school classmate—I stole the book from her while she went to the ladies' room, checked it out of the library, and left before she returned to her seat). I can tell you details about that book as well, not only because there are some crazy over-the-top moments but because that book made a tremendous impression on me. It was not just the story of two very headstrong (I believe the word "mule-headed" was used by both parties) people learning to accept one another, but the absolutely insane lengths the heroine, Frances, goes to to avoid marrying the hero. She goes from Hot Scottish Lassie to Butt-Ugly, Judgmental, Slightly Rumpled, Possibly Smelly, and Definitely Nearsighted Dowd—and he marries her anyway, precisely because he thinks she really is all of those things. Imagine his surprise when a few months later he discovers she's really quite lovely (read: hot), she's terribly intelligent, and she's wickedly and lastingly pissed off at him.

Reading this book, with the mistaken identity and the characters being hoisted by their own petards more than once, was a revelation to my fiction-starved teenage mind. Here were stories, big, rich, detailed, lengthy stories, about passion and excitement and places I'd never been. I was tired of stories about high schools that were populated by people more beautiful, more blonde, more aquamarine-eyed, well-adjusted, and wealthy than I was, and in romances, I found adventure, challenge, and emotional depth I hadn't experienced in fiction before. In short: Boo Yah!

Just about every romance reader I've ever spoken to can recall the first romance she read, and certainly the romance that hooked her on the genre. As Harlequin sees it, the first romance is a moment of passage, and can be a marker of coming-of-age due to the emotional experience of finding this rich and very well-populated form of narrative written mostly by women, for women, about women.

And it's not just "older women" or "women of a certain age." Romance readers are all ages, so you can chuck that stereotype of women in their graying years, wearing shabby sweatshirts with stained sweatpants, reading fat paperbacks, and surrounded by too many cats. Romance readers are young and old, and may have nothing in common except the books they read and the experience they gain from reading them.

> Just about every romance reader I've ever spoken to can recall the first romance she read.

The Romance Writers of America collects statistics on romance readers every year, and according to their 2009 figures

- Women comprise just over 90 percent of the romance readership.
- The majority of the readership in the United States is women ages thirty-one to forty-nine.
- Most romance readers are currently in a romantic relationship. (So maybe that theory that romance readers are desperate, single, undersexed neurotics can go away too. Please.)

Harlequin's research has revealed what they consider the three main things that we romance readers receive from our fiction-reading. The first is rather obvious: escape and relaxation—but, as Finlay says, those are broad and generic terms. Most people read anything to escape or relax. Romance specifically creates a sense of hope and hopefulness that a romantic situation can and does exist. Perhaps you haven't experienced it with your parent's marriage or your friends' marriages or your own relationships, but there is lasting romance. Romance reading affirms that idea and supports belief in the possibility.

Second, romance readers find ways to temporarily leave their present situations—though not every reader escapes entirely into the fantasy world. Certainly not every reader believes she is being kissed by a secret prince who is also a billionaire and a well-hung sexually adventurous tiger in the bedroom besides. The value of romance-reading, as Harlequin has found with its reader focus groups, is not so much in what the romance novel offers as an escape destination, but what reading offers as a temporary rest from the present stress and demands of life.

One woman in a focus group mentioned that her every waking moment was spent caring for her son, who was dying. The only time she had to forget that daily pain was when she was reading a romance, because then she could get away from that imminent unhappy ending.

It's not always a tragic situation that brings readers back to romance. Any amount of rest from a present stress could be desired. Another woman said that romances help her make that transition from workday to family evening: "I just need thirty minutes after work of reading Harlequin books and all the stress of the day is gone. All it takes is thirty minutes and then I'm ready to cook dinner." Escape and fantasy play an important role in every person's life, whether it's the fantasy of romance, or the fantasy of being an unstoppable warrior, or knowing you're the smartest person in the room, able to solve any puzzle with observational skills and the ability to quirk one eyebrow. The time spent in escape and fantasy, regardless of the venue of the escape, is fulfilling because it presents a time of rest and quiet while one is awake. Some people watch TV, some folks play games, some build or create things, and some people read—and some do all of the above, though not necessarily at the same time. One would hope not, anyway—might be messy.

A third benefit that romance readers receive, according to Harlequin's research (which I am told fills many a PowerPoint presentation), is the validation of seeing their lives, their stresses, their beliefs, and their values reflected in fictional narratives. It's reassuring to see confirmation of your own beliefs and to find someone or something that is like you. This is part of the reason that inspirational or Christian-focused romance is popular: it is reassuring for a reader to see a validation of personal values, and to realize that one is not a freak for wanting to attend church, for finding community in a spiritual setting, or for wanting to be chaste.

XO
XO

Within the romance genre, there exists the validation of the belief and the desire for a happy ending, and the idea of a perfect someone who will create happiness in tandem. Perhaps this explains why romance readers are in romantic relationships themselves: they're repeatedly reading about successful relationships, and creating ones for themselves as best they can.

This is not to say that every romance reader is in a happily blissful relationship—not true. Some are single, some are partnered and miserable, and some have a relationship that's in progress. But the affirmation of seeing conflict resolution and the acquisition of more self-confidence played out over and over again with different problems and different people can create a belief in the possibility that, if a fictional heroine can overcome that problem, surely one's own difficulties can be battled into submission. It's pretty simple: seeing kicking of ass inspires one to kick ass.

These benefits of reading romance, as Harlequin puts it, are only some of the reasons why romance readers are so devoted to the genre—and boy howdy, are we devoted. This dedication is one unique quirk of the romance reader. We turn to romances and stories of courtship again and again. We finish one book and immediately seek another. We read romances that vary in settings a few hundred years or even light-years apart from one another, but we return to the stories of courtship repeatedly.

One reason that fans of the romance genre read so much of it is that there are few experiences as thrilling as falling into an electric attraction or a feisty relationship with someone you're seriously, seriously into. Falling into like, into love, or even into oh-my-gosh-I-want-to-kiss-you is a heady and delicious experience.

Author Julia London says that her readers thank her for the ability to re-experience their joy and excitement through fiction: "They have thanked me for giving them a romance to fall into. I think that feeling of falling in love is something we have all experienced and for many of us, that falling in love has turned to companionable love. Yet the feeling of falling is something we want to experience again, and I think readers can do that safely in a book and keep the love without giving up the love we have. It's not that readers idolize the hero or heroine and wish their own spouse was more like that person. Reading romance is about the emotional attachment and connection, and enjoying that thrill in a contained narrative (one that guarantees a happy ending—don't forget that part)."

Reading about the emotional experience allows the reader to enjoy it vicariously, to feel the emotional pull and upheaval without going through it personally—which is a good thing because it can be exhausting! This isn't truly different from someone who adores thriller, spy, or crime novels because they enjoy being scared, or someone who reads fantasy or science fiction novels because they like the experience of being placed into an alternate universe and learning their way around each time they pick up a new book. That vicarious emotional and intellectual thrill is one reason people read and return to romance repeatedly. We see reflections of ourselves in romance, and of our own experiences, each time we read.

To quote French author François Mauriac, "'Tell me what you read and I'll tell you who you are' is true enough, but I'd know you better if you told me what you reread."

> "The feeling of falling in love is something we want to experience again, and I think readers can do that safely in a book... without giving up the love we have."
>
> —JULIA LONDON

SEEING YOURSELF IN A ROMANCE

Romance readers can find inspiration in their romance in myriad ways. Reba, a fan of the genre, says that one thing she enjoys "about romance novels is the [depiction of a] woman struggling for independence in a world that does not recognize her value. Historicals are especially good for this, but I think they only highlight things that women recognize exist to this day. To wit, even our literature is seen as 'less than,' despite strong writing, compelling storytelling, and regular inclusion of universal truths (or as universal as truths can get, anyway).

"So women fighting to be seen as strong, smart, fully real-ized human beings with something to offer strikes a chord with me. Since I do have the benefit of civil rights (such as they are) and a more open society (ditto), the least I can do is sally forth with as much pluck as the heroine of a Victorian novel, grateful that, if nothing else, I don't have to manage a bustle."

Seeing one's values and desires in a narrative is powerful—and so is seeing the possibility of one's ideal self. I realize that sounds tremendously Oprah-esque, but hear me out. Reading romances can and absolutely has taught readers to consider who they want to be, and has allowed them to understand themselves in a unique fashion.

It can be difficult to find realistic and possible encounters between two people in popular entertainment. The best storytelling combines the impossible drama, the improbable tension, and the realistic encounters that depict awkward and confusing human relations. Not everyone is in an impossibly exclusive private school for wealthy teens, or running for their lives from yet another serial killer, or being blackmailed into posing as a stunningly beautiful tycoon's mistress, or fighting vampires in Regency England. But everyone knows that feeling when you see something or someone you admire, and find yourself wanting to emulate. Seeing your potential ideal self, whether she is brave, clever, funny, or merely able to get through the awkward moment of not knowing what to say to someone, can be absorbing and inspiring.

On a long and entertaining thread of comments on my website, romance readers shared with me what they learned from romance, and how they learned about themselves from the books they've enjoyed—and the characters they've loved and hated.

Avid reader Kelly says she thinks romances help her envision her own future because they help her picture situations objectively and figure out what it was she wanted in a relationship: "Romances have helped me to think through things. How would I act in this situation, how would I react to that, would I put up with that, what would be a deal-breaker, what would I SAY? For example, would I move across the country to be with him? Would I take the chance of being able to find a new job that I like as much as my current one? Do I trust him to be alone with his ex? Do I care that he has a difficult kid? Would I want to be with a guy who has that much anger? Is he too controlling? Romances have put words to feelings and experiences. When the hero and heroine break up, you feel the pain, and when you feel it in real life, it's familiar and less scary. By acting out things in [my] imagination, I prepared for real life.

"Romance novels are over-the-top and exaggerated, completely focused on relationships, but that's what they are for. The relationship lessons are highlighted by being exaggerated."

> ### "Romances have helped me to think through things."
> —KELLY, A READER

Romance reader Nadia says romance has absolutely taught her how she would like to be valued: "I'd say being a lover of romances from early high school on did help me in relationships as a barometer of what I did or didn't want. The heroines of favorite romances have one thing in common: they are worth the effort. And so, eventually, that seeped into my own thinking.

"Maybe he won't have to save me from pirates, or disguise himself to secretly marry me to rescue me from a worse fate, or deliberately lose a major football game to keep me from getting killed by the villain, but dammit, he could make a date and keep it, wash the sheets before I spend the night, and cook dinner every now and then."

I love how she expressed that idea: the heroine is worth the effort, no matter how insane and complicated that effort may be—and let's be honest, there are some crazy situations that romance heroes and heroines have to dig themselves out of before they can reach the final pages and their happy-ever-after.

Olivia T. says similarly that romances have taught her about herself: "I did not start reading romance novels until after the end of my First Real Relationship. At first they were a comfort to me, reminding me that I was well rid of that idiot because he sure did not act like any of the heroes in the books I was reading.

"However, after reading more romance novels I found that romance is not about a perfect man meeting a perfect woman and living happily ever after...It isn't about meeting a perfect man; it's about meeting the man who is perfect for me. Romance has taught me to own myself."

We interrupt this nonfictional celebration of romance to bring you...*romance!* Sprinkled throughout the book are excerpts from romances that illustrate the points I'm making, and represent some of the very best of the genre. Enjoy, and if you need a shopping list, there's one in the back.

Mr. Turner slid his finger under her chin. "Yet another reason why I am glad I am not a gentleman. Do you know why my peers want their brides to have pale skin?"

She was all too aware of the golden glow of vitality emanating from him. She could feel the warmth in his finger. She shouldn't encourage him. Still, the word slipped out. "Why?"

"They want a woman who is a canvas, white and empty. Standing still, existing for no other purpose than to serve as a mute object onto which they can paint their own hopes and desires. They want their brides veiled. They want a demure, blank space they can fill with whatever they desire."

He tipped her chin up, and the afternoon sunlight spilled over the rim of her bonnet, touching her face with warmth.

"No." Margaret wished she could snatch that wavering syllable back. But what he said was too true to be borne, and nobody knew it better than she. Her own wants and desires had been insignificant. She'd been engaged to her brother's friend before her second season had been halfway over. She'd been a pale, insipid nothing, a collection of rites of etiquette and rules of precedent squashed into womanly form and given a dowry.

His voice was low. "Damn their bonnets. Damn their rules."

"What do you want?" Her hands were shaking. "Why are you doing this to me?"

"Miss Lowell, you magnificent creature, I want you to paint your own canvas. I want you to unveil yourself." He raised his hand to her cheek and traced the line of warm sunshine down her jaw. That faint caress was hotter and more dizzying than the relentless sun over-head. She stood straight, not letting herself respond, hoping that her cheeks wouldn't flush.

—*UNVEILED* BY COURTNEY MILAN, 2011

Romance shows us that you have to look out for yourself first, and place the quest for someone else as a secondary concern to your own happiness. This is one aspect of romance novels that many people who don't read them don't quite get: at no time is anyone sitting around waiting for Lord Wonderful and His Majestic Pants to come galloping in on a giant (yet well-behaved) horse to sweep the heroine off her feet and into a blissfully purple and fuchsia happy-ever-after. Hell to the no.

No matter what you may have heard, romance novel heroines are not unilaterally selfless, spineless wimps who achieve a backbone only after being introduced to the erect specimen of manly achievement and consequence that is the hero. You might encounter a doormat heroine, but she is not the quintessential heroine any more. In fact, one thing you must know about romance readers is that we aren't that impressed with novels featuring women who do nothing until the hero shows up. The most negative romance reviews on any website or online bookstore are frequently directed at books featuring a heroine with no spine to speak of.

Romance novels often feature women who are already accomplished and men who are relatively happy in their own lives as well. Romances featuring people who pine for someone, anyone who will do everything to make them happy, well, those aren't romances. To quote the romantic comedy *The Holiday*: "You're supposed to be the leading lady of your own life, for God's sake!" If a person who is content with his life meets someone who makes everything just a little bit more challenging, who both fits and doesn't fit into his life and his routine, to quote Guy Fieri, it is On Like Donkey Kong: swing the rope, jump the barrel, and save the princess.

> ### "Romance has taught me to own myself."
> —OLIVIA T., A READER

If you get nothing else from this chapter, or this entire book, let it be that romance novels, to quote Olivia, help readers own themselves and learn to become a heroine worth her own happy ending.

Romances can also help readers fix some not-so-attractive habits. Caroline writes that romances have helped her identify potentially crappy habits of her own: "There were some books that taught me just how stupid some behaviours are. I recognized my own actions in what the heroine was doing. When I stopped reading, I slapped my forehead and exclaimed 'Wow, she's a (insert descriptive of asshattery here).' I stopped and went 'but, but, but…I done did that with Mr. X. Oh s★★★!' I knew that if I read it and it sounded dumb to do, maybe, just maybe, I shouldn't [do it] either?"

Amber G. also figured out some basics of interpersonal relationships from really annoying plot devices: "Romance taught me…that passive aggressive behaviour is aggravating. Nobody ends up happy when someone is upset

> ## "Relationships are about compromise."
>
> —EVE SAVAGE

and then waits for the other person to read their mind, getting angry when this obviously never happens."

Merriam has had an identical experience: "When the 'big misunderstanding' in a story is caused by a failure to communicate, it not only annoys me but it reminds me to try and be more open and to talk more about what the issue is, or what is going on in my real life. I am also much clearer about what I am looking for in the other person because I have tried on for size the heroes in romance stories. I also think you can't underestimate the role of redemption in romance novels, with their message that we all get things wrong and must consciously work on fixing what is broken."

Romances also teach that the heroine can be strong and that sex is not the only method through which to achieve intimacy, nor is it always the advisable or even the safest choice. Erotica author Eve Savage says that romances have helped her define what makes for a strong relationship—and what makes for an adventurous relationship as well: "Romances have definitely had an impact in my life. I didn't start reading them until later (early to mid '90s), and by then they'd evolved from the 'wimpy heroine/raping hero' style to the 'confident but flawed heroine/strong yet sensitive hero' style. This enabled me to realize relationships are about compromise. They helped me understand I was worth something and that most important lesson—sex does not equal love."

Savage is not the only person who discovered and explored her own self-worth and relationships through the writing of romances. A writer who wished to remain anonymous and went by the name "anonapotamus," thereby earning a huge giggle and my respect forever, writes that it wasn't reading romance but writing romance that helped her slowly realize that her marriage was not ideal and that she deserved better for herself: "The more I learned about crafting stories, the more I told myself, 'It's a fantasy—this isn't how real guys think and act; it's how we (women) want to believe they think and act.' And I convinced myself that what I had was as good as it was going to get. More, I think somewhere deep down inside, I kept waiting to get through the bad times to the big payoff on the other side.

....

"I am also much clearer about what I am looking for in the other person because I have tried on for size the heroes in romance stories."—MERRIAM, A READER

....

"Twelve years, thirty-plus books, and some therapy later, I'm newly single, happier than I've been in a long time, and ready to Not Fucking Settle this time around. In the meantime, I've got a career I love and family, writer friends, and wonderful stories to keep me company."

Another writer who goes by the name Odette Lovegood

used romance to help her overcome her own shyness when she met someone she was tremendously interested in—and who was just as shy. But instead of reading it, she and her boyfriend collaborate on fiction with strong romance plotlines: "Writing romance allowed us to get to know one another and express our feelings in ways we never could have otherwise. It got me in touch with my own sexuality, and made me realize that sex isn't something to be afraid of."

Reader and writer Sarah W. (no, not me) says that the books she read helped her figure out what kind of person she didn't want to be with—and figure out the goals for her own parenting: "Oddly enough, the rape-y, obsessive, I-hate-you-because-I-love-you, he-loves-me-so-it's-okay romances that were popular (or at least crowded the shelves at the library and the used bookstore) when I was growing up showed me how wrong that sort of behavior is. My own characters (female or male) don't stand for that—or don't by the end of the story. And I'm raising my kids to know that real love is so much more than…drama and that they're worth so much more."

WHO WERE THESE RAPETASTIC ASSCLOWN HEROES?

Once upon a time, not so far behind us, romance novels were often populated by heroes who would be a half-step from a restraining order today. They were autocratic, they were self-important, and their goal was to break the maidenhead of the heroine, often by force or forced seduction, such as overwhelming her with assertive sexual conduct until the poor, overwrought, confused thing could no longer think for herself. Think of it as the historical equivalent of a roofie, only written in purple prose. If this sounds miserable, well, it often was. These are what we call Old Skool romances. The focus of the Old Skool romance is most often the heroine, because the stories were mostly about her journey to self-discovery and orgasms described in terminology usually reserved for natural phenomena. The heroines of Old Skool romances are often helpless under the influence of the alpha male assholes (whom we call alpholes), and while these books reflected the sexual ambivalence of the time in which they were published, they are not always popular with romance readers today.

Caroline, another eager romance reader, agrees that identifying behavior that repulses you in fictional portrayals makes it a lot damn easier to spot it in real life: "Romance novels taught me it is never OK to let a man take advantage of you. I was so turned off in my early reading years with the 'force my mighty sword-o-lovin' on you and you will love and loathe me for it' storyline. Ick. I remember never allowing a guy to just slobber and grope his way about without my explicit permission, remembering how awful it sounded when I read scenes such as that. The 'I can't stop, I'm so in lust and out of control for you' line never worked on me. A knee to your groin will help then, right? Romance novels [also] taught me it is OK to fantasize, and dream, and take pleasure in someone else's happy ending without needing to compare my own happy ending, or dejectedly pine that my romantic life sucks. It's fiction, it's fantasy, and it's healthy, but it's not real."

"Romance novels taught me it is never OK to let a man take advantage of you."—CAROLINE, A READER

Emotions are tricky, and, as *Smart Bitches* cofounder Candy Tan wrote in our book *Beyond Heaving Bosoms: The Smart Bitches' Guide to Romance Novels*, we are, especially in the United States, taught early that emotions are squicky, uncomfortable things that should not be talked about and certainly not displayed too much. Some people are very skilled at dampening their own emotions, and the safe harbor of reading romance and knowing that the emotional response you might feel for the characters or the story will end happily and without loss or grief is an equally safe space to explore emotions one might not otherwise want to feel at all. One reader, Em, writes, "I'm a fairly emotionally dead person when it comes to real life, so fiction gives me people I can care about without the pain that caused my apathy in the first place. Romance novels—being so emotionally charged—are the best for that."

Amber G. is a shy person who figured out with the help of romance novels how she might interact with people she doesn't know: "The first thing romance as a genre did for me was teach me about flirting. It was romance that taught me how to smile, how to meet someone's eyes, that relaxing was good and so was dressing nicely and looking as though I cared."

....

> "The first thing romance did for me was teach me about flirting. It was romance that taught me how to smile."—AMBER G., A READER

....

Jill Q. says, "I think what romances taught me was that it was OK to feel and have positive emotions, to be an optimist not just about love, but about anything. I think romance, like all genre fiction, generally has a positive message. You can stop the evil overlord, catch the murderer, fall in love. Be proactive about your life and good things will happen."

Amanda M. says that when she was reading romances as a teen, "it was quite reassuring to read the 'plain girl gets the guy' stories. I was just entering that very awful awkward stage with gaining weight in the wrong places, gaining in the right place but not being ready for it, pimples, and all that other stuff. I was not only an ugly duckling, but a shy, lonely duckling. But I read books where the heroine was sometimes plump and plain, yet her intelligence and sweetness earned her love from a good man. It helped me to keep believing that even if I wasn't the beautiful, vivacious prom queen, I still deserved and could find someone who loved me without a miraculous makeover."

"You look good," Cal said, with enough tension in his voice to make it an understatement.

"It's not a fat dress," Min said, turning back to the mirror. "It doesn't hide anything."

"Haven't we talked about this?" Cal said, coming to stand behind her.

"Yes, but my mother has talked since then," Min said. "Also, there's this mirror which tells me I don't have much of a waistline."

"You have a waistline." Cal put his hands on her hips. "It's right here." He slid his hands across her stomach and she shivered, watching him touch her in the mirror. With Cal's hands on her, she looked different, good, and when he pulled her back against his chest, she relaxed into him and let her head fall back on his shoulder. "Very sexy dress," he whispered into her ear, and then kissed her neck. She drew in her breath and he whispered, "Very sexy woman," and moved his hand up to her neckline, drawing his finger down the edge of the silky fabric, making her shudder as the heat spread and she began to feel liquid everywhere.

"I have to stop drinking wine when I'm with you," she whispered to him in the mirror. "I start believing all this garbage you tell me."

—*BET ME* BY JENNIFER CRUSIE, 2008

In addition to owning ourselves, romance novels teach women to be confident in our strengths. Reading about heroines who have a continual need to please gets old, unless that heroine learns to please herself first. Selflessness is not an admirable trait when it means you give away everything about yourself, and that includes both men and women. I'm not saying selfishness is the key to being heroic—it surely is not. But molding yourself to the expectations of others is not heroic either, and misleads everyone, including you, and makes for a heroine about as exciting and passionate as plain yogurt at room temperature.

> The trick to being the heroine of your own story is being happy with who you are. Confidence and accomplishment are hot damn sexy.

Certainly women are bombarded with messages that they should achieve perfection in the eyes of everyone around them, but the same messages are sent to men as well. The trick to being the heroine of your own story is being happy with who you are. Confidence and accomplishment are hot damn sexy.

Just as there is no one single type of romance novel, there is no one way to read romance, and there's no one way that readers use their romance-reading. Women read romance and bring it into their lives in many, many different ways. Identifying their own likes, desires, and senses of worth—and of being worth the effort so they don't feel the need to settle for less than what they want—is only part of the value of romance for the reader.

Happiness, much like something spilling in the fridge, has a trickle-down effect, only much less sticky.

In addition to knowing ourselves, we also know happiness, and romance makes readers happy in a myriad of ways.

Now, this is not to say that romance readers are unhappy. They are not miserable and seeking panacea and palliative emotional fluffing in their reading. Most romance readers are happy already—and their reading material increases their joy and allows them to bring it to others. Would you rather have your dinner with your happy mom or your unhappy mom, your happy wife or your unhappy wife? Happiness, much like something spilling in the fridge, has a trickle-down effect, only much less sticky.

Romance readers bring their romance to life as they read it and find happiness, and they bring that happiness to their lives after they're done reading. As Harlequin's research has revealed, romance readers give themselves the gifts of time, quiet, peace, and hopeful optimism as they read—and they bring those gifts to others. In doing so, they recognize themselves and find validation and affirmation for their own desire for happiness.

And, equally important, after they learn to identify what they want in a relationship, they learn they can and will find it.

We Know More Than
a Few Good Men

·············· ♥ ··············

Ah, romance heroes. If you judge the books by their covers (and really, I can't tell you enough that you shouldn't be doing that), then you have a pretty powerful, well-muscled idea of what a romance hero should look like. In fact, copying the appearance of a romance novel cover model is not that difficult, provided you can work out for many, many hours, eat lean protein, and flex your biceps and abdominal wall for hours on end.

Once you've acquired the musculature, which only takes a few unending months of nonstop bodybuilding, the payoff is that the rest is easy.

SIX SIMPLE STEPS TO LOOKING LIKE THE QUINTESSENTIAL ROMANCE HERO

STEP 1
Acquire a mullet.

STEP 2
Spend an uncommonly long time working on the style, shine, and bounceability of that mullet.

STEP 3
Don't let anyone but the heroine touch your mullet. (That is not a euphemism. No, wait, it could be.)

STEP 4
Maintain a state of partial undress wherein your shirt is unbuttoned but still tucked in.

STEP 5
Ensure that the wind is buffeting your manly chestular landscape in as flattering a manner as possible.

STEP 6
Be careful of your strategically placed weapon. Sometimes, ok, a lot of the time, there is a gun pointed business-end-down in the waistband of your pants. Or, perhaps there's a sword, unsheathed, of course, along side your femoral artery. All I'm saying is, be careful. You'll put your eye out.

In reality, the most common image of romance manhood as depicted on the covers is as ridiculous as the idea that mullets were ever a solid fashion choice for one's hair. And because of the over-the-top, top-heavy images of males in romance, one of the most common accusations tossed in the direction of readers is that all that romance reading gives women unrealistic expectations of love, of sex, and of men in general. Too much romance and we readers will expect our men to be as muscled as the men on the covers, as well-coiffed and overdeveloped and as clueless about normal shirt wearing as the average model. That visual perfection of the cover has, unfortunately, intimidated more than one mortal male, who thought that the men inside were as outsized and overly perfect as the depiction on the cover.

Once again: deep-fried bullpucky.

Let me get the obvious hero business out of the way first:

Romance readers do not expect real men to closely echo and emulate the heroes of our nearest romance novel. No, not even that one, with the buns so tight you could bounce a yak off his left buttock.

Really.

It is true that sometimes the male characters are idealized, and the sex is sometimes—okay, frequently—idealized. More importantly, the male depicted on the cover more often than not bears no resemblance to the hero of the story itself. But readers can tell the difference between fantasy and reality when it comes to actual human males—and they're smart enough to know how the fantasy can educate and inform their own reality. Nowhere is this more obvious than with men.

> We do not expect real men to look like the men on our books.

Men in romance novels, to quote my husband, are not real

dudes. Real dudes don't usually think about their emotions as much as heroes do in a novel. Most real dudes do not sit and ruminate for hours about their attraction to a person or analyze their feelings. Whether it's cultural inculcation or gender difference—and my money is on the former, not the latter—men aren't going to spend a few pages' worth of narration pondering their deep and abiding emotional bond with a woman.

This is not to say that men do not have feelings. They absolutely do—but since emotional display is unseemly at best and emasculating at worst, particularly among men in most cultures, there aren't always going to be those deep and squishy moments as there are in romances.

But improbable muscles, deep emotional pondering, and squishy feelings aside, real romance heroes are everywhere. We're not all looking for pirate kings who are secretly dukes, or tycoons of unspecified industry who need someone to pose as their fiancée to close a tricky business deal. We know these men don't exist in plentiful supply, much less at all.

But we do know that there are many good men (and women) out there, and most of us, since most romance readers are in relationships, have already found one. We can separate reality from ridiculous, fact from fiction, and find real-life men who are real-life romance heroes, in small and magnificent moments.

Note: I am speaking specifically about men in this chapter, but by no means are all romance fans heterosexual. Many are lesbian or gay individuals. By writing about male heroes, I do not mean to imply that only heterosexual people read romance, nor that romance can only take place between heterosexual couples. Heroism exists in both genders; in this chapter I'm speaking specifically about male stereotypes, archetypes, and daguerreotypes. Okay, not that last one, but you get the point.

The appearance of the romance hero, all muscled and mullety, is not the reality of the romance hero. The romance hero can be found in just about anyone. For example, as I write this, my husband has taken our two children to a Disney children's show, *ON ICE*, so that I would have total quiet and isolation in which to work. That is a romance hero. I hear he is possibly eating a flavored ice out of Jessie the Cowgirl's head, much like devouring icy cold BRAAAAINS.

Little moments assembled together make the romance hero. The man who brings you a drink after a very long and brain-frazzling day or who walks through the door, sees you on your last moment of patience, and turns around to fetch take-out for dinner—that's a romance hero. The man who holds a door, who notices you need a hand, or who shows up to simply be there when you're facing something difficult—that's a romance hero.

As an article in the *Boston Globe* in October 2009 by oncologist Robin Schoenthaler stated, the ideal man is not the one with the biggest bank account or the extreme sports habit, but is the man who will hold your purse in the cancer clinic:

"I became acquainted with what I've come to call great 'purse partners' at a cancer clinic in Waltham. Every day these husbands drove their wives in for their radiation treatments, and every day these couples sat side by side in the waiting room, without much fuss and without much chitchat. Each wife, when her name was called, would stand, take a breath, and hand her purse over to her husband. Then she'd disappear into the recesses of the radiation room, leaving behind a stony-faced man holding what was typically a white vinyl pocketbook. On his lap. The guy—usually retired from the trades, a grandfather a dozen times over, a Sox fan since date of conception—sat there silently with that purse. He didn't read, he didn't talk, he just sat there with the knowledge that twenty feet away technologists were preparing to program an unimaginably complicated X-ray machine and aim it at the mother of his kids.

"I'd walk by and catch him staring into space, holding hard onto the pocketbook, his big gnarled knuckles clamped around the clasp, and think, 'What a prince.'"

OUR FAVORITE ROMANCE HEROES

Is there a difference between real-life heroes and romance-novel heroes? Le Duh. Of course there is. But beneath the stereotypical imagery and the unfortunate typecasting that men in fiction and in entertainment endure, there are real men who are romance heroes. It may be so traditional it's almost cliché to joke about men who don't do dishes or help with house-work or even actively parent—but more often than not, men are strong and worthy partners and are the exception to that demeaning stereotype. And as I said earlier, we do not expect men to look like the men on our books. But that doesn't mean we don't and shouldn't expect men to at times act like the heroes of our books. Fortunately, so many of them do.

Every romance reader has a favorite type of hero or a favorite character. As I wrote on the website awhile back, my favorite heroes are a mix. Sometimes I love reading the abidingly constant loving man with horny-pants, often portrayed as waiting for the heroine to wake up and realize he is perfect for her, but not sure what to do with his feelings in the meantime. Other times I adore reading the "I don't like you, you drive me nuts, I can't stop thinking about your hair, DAMMIT!" hero.

> The ideal man is not the one with the biggest bank account or the extreme sports habit, but is the man who will hold your purse in the cancer clinic.

One hero I love rereading is Ethan from the Nora Roberts Chesapeake Bay series. Yet I would *totally* be wary of him in real life. Quiet but intense is fun to read about: *"What's going on under the surface? I can't tell—a puzzle! Fun!"* The same character is not so fun in real life: *"I know there's something going on under the surface but I can't read what it is. It's a mystery…that makes him possibly creepy."*

What do I learn from reading about Ethan, who is a very damaged and yet very honorable hero? What do I learn about real people while reading about a fictional person? I learn that a person can change and outgrow a painful past that's cut by abuse and cruelty, and I learn that as much as someone might prefer not to have feelings at all and try to suppress them, the experience of good feelings—or really, really, really good feelings—is worth the pain and trouble of dealing with all those other pesky emotions. I learn the value and power of loyalty, and how families can be made when you're an adult.

All valuable lessons and, in my opinion, important things to know about people that I might not otherwise have understood without that fictional portrayal. That's the nice thing about romances: real emotions and, in the hands of a skilled writer, almost-real people, existing in totally fictional circumstances.

Most romance readers have a favorite hero, or heroes, and the reason why that hero is a favorite is often revealing—as is the fact that readers share many common favorites. When I asked the readers of my site which types of heroes they adored, the answers were not as varied as I'd expected—though this is by far only a small sampling of the many, many flavors of romance hero out there for your reading pleasure.

THE CARE-GIVING ALPHA MALE

Kati loves the care-giving alpha male, "who is all kinds of dominant, but spends pretty much every moment after meeting the heroine trying to take care of her—usually to varying degrees of success." I love this type of hero too, usually because he is all kinds of irritated with that impulse to take care of someone to the exclusion of other tasks, and that will cue that "I don't want to like you, I can't stop thinking about your hair, DAMMIT!" frustration.

Kati's favorite hero of this type: "Jack Travis from Lisa Kleypas's *Smooth Talking Stranger*. Pretty much from the instant Ella accuses him of being her nephew's father, he is trying to take care of her, either by finding her a place to live, facilitating her meeting with a high-powered player in Houston, or putting together the baby's crib. He's completely alpha, but he cannot stop taking care of her. And woos her, and the reader, as he goes."

Liza the Evil Twin agrees: "In addition to what Kati so eloquently stated, I love how relentless Jack is in pursuit of Ella. Not in a crazy, stalker-ish way, but in his focus on *her* needs, desires, concerns, and happiness. Plus, he is so fun-loving, and has such a wicked, smart-ass sense of humor that just slays me."

Jack Travis is a great example of how being an alpha male doesn't mean you have to be an asshole to everyone around you. Alpha males in the new vernacular don't put up with a lot of crap from anyone, but they also know how to be careful, and caring, without compromising themselves or their strength. Too often, people who aren't familiar with romance presume that reading about alpha males means that women are reading and therefore fantasizing about men who do little but treat them badly, and sometimes cruelly. Not true, and not so. Alpha males from Old Skool romance, most commonly found in the '70s and '80s, with a little unfortunate leakage into the early '90s, are definitely hurtful and unyielding, unbending, and even sometimes cruel to the heroine.

Romances today portray men as equal partners in the development and upkeep of a happy relationship. One of the hallmarks of the romance genre now (as opposed to those early romances of the '70s and '80s, more commonly referred to as "bodice rippers"—so named because often, a bodice was ripped in the course of unwilling seduction) is that the hero has to earn his happy ending. Much like the stereotypical wedding preparation, where the bride loses her mind over cocktail napkin colors and the groom just has to show up in a tuxedo at the right time, the Old Skool romance hero just had to show up to be a catalyst for the heroine's readiness for romance heroine-hood. He didn't have to change very much to win the girl and enjoy the happily ever after. He just had to be present at the right moments and be patient. Sometimes. Patience wasn't necessarily a trait commonly found in Old Skool heroes.

Now, heroes have to complete their own emotional journey and be active participants in the creation of the happy ending. They have to earn it. To quote RuPaul: "You better work." It's a lot of responsibility and there are admirable traits that must be present or develop during the story in order to achieve that happy ending.

The contemporary alpha that is most commonly found in romances published today is never without compassion or some glimmer of redemption. Confidence is required, as is strength—both moral and sometimes physical—and a backbone of unbreakable durability, but the hero who would force his will, or his body, on a heroine is a figment of the past (thank GOODNESS) in romance. Now, alpha heroes are of the mold that Kati and others like: strong, unbending, but capable of compassion. As Tracey Devlyn writes of her favorite heroes: "the hero cherished the heroine." A man is not going to do harm to someone who is valuable to him.

WHAT MAKES AN EXCELLENT ALPHA MALE HERO?

- Strength
- Compassion
- Confidence
- Moral code
- Commitment
- Loyalty
- Outstanding bedside manner (if you know what I mean, and I think you do)

THE HEROES WHO TACKLE AND LEARN
FROM THEIR PROBLEMS

A reader writing as Kitten says that the heroes she likes best "are the ones who have issues of their own. But also those who are willing to do something about it and who have a bit of a problem confronting the idea that they depend on someone else for their happiness. Some of the heroes in Stephanie Laurens's Cynsters' saga are like that—for example, Richard from *Scandal's Bride*, who has to take a secondary place in the estate of his wife. He has to adapt and become a partner instead of being a 'dictator'…Troubled, but willing to recover, and caring are the two best words to define what I like in my heroes."

A reader going by the name Sugarless says that, like me, she has "a soft spot for nerds in fiction, so guys like Carter from the first book of Nora Roberts Bride Quartet, *Vision in White*, is totally squee-worthy. I can love his frustration and uselessness at the whole dating rituals thing—since he expresses it with humor, it's adorable.

"I think this kind of guy would be a good boyfriend, but, unlike fiction, these guys in real life tend to be easily intimidated and are never sure what to do with my slightly neurotic self. Also—too many of them are too concerned with being a 'good boyfriend' to just be themselves. I mean, good on them for trying to be good to their girlfriends, but it's not going to last if he can't relax enough just to be himself. You find one that can, though, and I'm sure you've found a winner."

THE HEROES WHO RECOGNIZE THEIR
OWN WORTH—HONESTLY

A very awesome reader named saltypepper just finished reading a romance that revealed what a hero is: "I just finished *Ripping the Bodice* by Inara Lavey which I must mention because--**SPOILERS AHOY!**--Connor wins over Cassandra by pointing out that she only wants Rafael because he *looks* like the hero in a romance novel, whereas Connor, who doesn't, is willing to *act* like one because that's what she wants. If that is not a willingness to do what it takes to please his woman, I don't know what is. Plus, a man who's familiar enough with romances to know what kind of hero his heroine wants? Oh yeah. Lemme at him."

A moral core of strength and certainty appeals to Tinpantithesis (can I mention how much I love the names of the people who talk with me online? Seriously. Love), who says that she really loves "The Frustrated Do-Gooder. I have a weakness for Lawful Good or Chaotic Good Guys—people intent on helping others or making the world a better place. Doctors, hotshot lawyers, knights errant, always sticking up for the little guy and doing the right thing.

"Except they're not cheerful while doing it. When confronted with the ugly realities and inequalities of the real world, they get really irritated. Why are the dumb bureaucrats/corporate fat-cats/evil sorcerers/ Vulcan hobgoblins making it more difficult to help people? It's enough to make a guy short-tempered, foul-mouthed, and just plain ornery. But underneath the cynical exterior is a heart that loves people, lost causes, and of course, the heroine."

DreadPirateRachel says that she loves heroes "who appear to be bad boys in the beginning, but whom the heroines discover are unusually caring and gentle, even if they're not the most sensitive of beings. Heroes like C.L. from Jennifer Crusie's *Tell Me Lies*. He was a bad boy in high school, and heroine Maddie just can't believe that he might have changed in fifteen years. His frustration with trying to convince her to trust him is endearing, and Maddie has a legitimate reason to drag her heels (for once). I love watching the trust grow between the hero and heroine while simultaneously finding a deeper understanding of the hero's character.

"How much do I love this kind of hero? I married one."

Jane says that what matters most to her "in a hero is confidence in himself and in his heroine. That's why my favorite heroes tend to be guys like Clay and Lucas (from Kelley Armstrong's Women of the Otherworld series) or Zoë Archer's heroes. They always have their heroines' backs, but at the same time they trust them to take care of themselves.

"I like the guy who respects a woman's abilities, and thinks it's hot that she can kick ass. Plus I think these character types tend to have a more equitable/trusting relationship, which makes me more likely to believe in their happily-ever-after."

THE MYSTERY HERO

Another heroic type that readers enjoy is the hero who isn't what he appears to be. For various reasons, heroes in novels often hide their true personalities and appearances, such as pretending to be less intelligent than they really are. Heroes like these allow the reader to see more beneath the superficial disguise presented to the world of the novel. E. D. Walker calls these "idiot heroes," and says that there is "something so wonderful about seeing past the surface of someone, past the 'idiot' to the wonderful, perhaps selectively intelligent man, beneath."

Heroes can overcome significant personal obstacles to be hero-worthy. One character who fits that mold is fan-favorite Reggie Davenport from Mary Jo Putney's *The Rake*. Reggie was the villain in previous novels in Putney's series, but as reader Newf Herder says, when Reggie became the hero, it was at significant personal cost, and personal effort, because Reggie had to recover not only from his own villainous choices but his alcoholism: "Reggie is not perfect by any stretch, but he is so very real. He's a man capable of great things, in life and in love, once he finally surrenders himself. What I really liked was that he knew that he had to get sober for himself, and went for true recovery rather than being 'redeemed' or 'saved' by falling in love. Oh, and his heroine wears breeches! I'm always a fan of that."

Heroic traits can be complex. Alpha males are often dominant and can easily pass the boundaries of decent behavior to become domineering and insensitive, and emerge as an "alphole" hero, as we described in *Beyond Heaving Bosoms*, instead of an alpha hero. Alphole heroes are just domineering assholes disguising themselves as alpha males. Real alpha males don't need to be assholes. Dominance and confidence can be expressed in different ways that make them more appealing. Betty Fokker (another of my favorite reader pseudonyms) writes, "I like an alpha male, but he's gotta want a really feisty woman…not to dominate, but to admire and help. I loved, loved, loved Shane from *Agnes and the Hitman* by Jennifer Crusie and Bob Mayer, because he killed people yet still got her the air-conditioning unit of her dreams. Plus, she was prone to attempted murder. Which he liked in a woman."

ALL THOSE HEROES ARE HELPING US OUT

What do we romance readers know about men from our tales of courtship? Plenty. Our ability to recognize heroism is revealed by the heroes we like to read about, even if those are men that in reality we wouldn't be terribly interested in. It's also empowering and almost a secretive kind of research to witness different relationships with very different individuals developing, as it teaches the reader what is and isn't attractive—an entirely subjective and personal experience. We learn what we like, what we don't, and what possibilities exist, both in relationships and in individuals.

Reader Elirhe writes that "I might even say that romance novels also played a role in the development of my feminist beliefs: some of my first romance reads at the age of eleven were those old love = rape novels of the late '70s and '80s, and from the start, I knew those 'romances' were just wrong—I instinctively sensed that a) no man has the right to dominate a woman like that and pass it off as affection, and b) women should stand up for themselves and demand that they be treated as full human beings."

Natalie Arloa says that her husband's understanding of her love for romance helped her recognize what a truly good man he was: "It isn't that a particular romance novel has helped my relationship with my husband, but it was his complete acceptance of the fact that I read them that helped. I used to be a closet reader; I'd buy a category on a night I knew my husband would be out late (which was regularly, since he's a musician) and read it in that evening. If he came home early, I'd hide it under my pillow. And I kept them in a spot he never looked.

"We'd been married for seven years before he saw me read a romance novel, and that's mostly because I started getting longer contemporaries from the library and couldn't always put them down. He was nonplussed that I'd hidden them from him all those years. I felt so secure in his love for me as me and not an idea or certain expectations he might have for me—it was freeing."

Author Carrie Lofty knows that the secret to her marriage

was sharing obscure interests: "Fourteen years ago I was in England for my junior year abroad. An acquaintance and his two friends invited me to go out dancing. During the taxi ride to the club, one bloke chatted me up, one talked to the driver...and one ignored me. He was too busy staring out the window, conducting a mumbled argument with the radio DJ. After a night of dancing, he and I wound up talking about Imperial Russian history. I married him nine months later. I'll take 'indie kid history nerd' for the win."

....

"Since many romance readers encounter romance for the first time in high school, which is not as a rule populated with kind and self-aware people of any gender, knowing that there are good people in the world at large can be very reassuring."—JILL Q, A READER

....

Editor Angela James says that romance novels themselves helped her identify the best possible man for her: "I was sitting on the couch, reading. I don't remember the book but I remember it was a romance (with a clinch cover!) and my then-fiancé got incredibly upset. He started saying how much he hated that I was always reading, and he wished I wouldn't read so much. He even mentioned that he especially hated that

I read 'those' books (you know, romances). I can't dramatically say that was the beginning of the end for us, but I eventually did decide a few years later that I wasn't going to marry him, and it's clear that what he said, how he felt, made an impression on me. I felt, at the time, and still do, that someone who loved me would understand that reading, and romances, were a part of who I am. You don't get me without the romances.

"Josh, my husband now? He totally gets that. It helps that my 'hobby' turned into my career, but he's that guy who speaks proudly of his wife being a bookworm and who says he hopes our daughter 'takes after me.' Now that is romantic. And so, with the help of romances, it's easy to see which is Prince Charming, and which is the frog."

Wednesday, a reader, had a horrible relationship, but romances have helped her believe that better men are out there: "By the time I got out of it, I felt broken. I didn't really believe in love any more, period.

"I think I started reading romance novels because part of me wanted to hold on to the belief that things could be different. It was comforting to read about couples where the man was actually interested in and appreciated the woman.

"It was reassuring to read about sex as something that could be mutual and enjoyable, not boundary-pushing and innovative. I know perfectly well that they're fictional and that if I have another relationship, it won't be storybook, but I think romance novels have helped me rebuild a healthier ideal of what a relationship should be."

Readers can learn that there are different men out there

from the ones they may have known personally. As reader Jill Q. says, "I was a plain nerdy girl in a small town. The majority of the boys I met in high school were neither kind nor bright. I had to hold out hope that there were good men out there, not just for me but for the sake of the population at large.

"Since many romance readers encounter romance for the first time in high school, which is not as a rule populated with kind and self-aware people of any gender, knowing that there are good people in the world at large can be very reassuring. That which is held up as 'heroic' in high school can be very different from that which is 'heroic' as an adult, most notably demonstrating sexual and personal respect for one another, and one's self."

Reading about different types of people and different and sometimes impossible situations gives romance readers a better understanding of what they want in a relationship. Romances can also teach you what not to want, just as cable TV can teach you what not to wear, what house not to buy, and what food not to cook—and what wine not to drink (trust me, though, some wine in a box is fantastic and you should feel no shame about that!).

THE TOP NINE ROMANCE HEROES

Nine? Yes, nine. Why nine? Because any list about the best hero is bound to be greeted with "But what about…" and "You forgot…" So, in order to head off (ha!) those protests, there are only nine, leaving one space for your personal favorite hero. Consider it your write-in candidate space—and feel free to email me at sarah@smartbitchestrashybooks.com to tell me your choice for the tenth man to finish the Top Romance Heroes list.

So who are the top nine heroes among romance readers? It's a list under much dispute, but culled from the discussions on Twitter and on varying websites, the top reader favorite heroes (for today, anyway—it could easily change tomorrow) are…

MILES VORKOSIGAN
The Vorkosigan Saga
By Lois McMaster Bujold

Bujold's series is science fiction, not romance, but her protagonist Miles Vorkosigan is a most beloved character, which is curious not only because of his location just out-side the romance genre, but because he has a story arc that takes place over several books. What makes Miles so fasci-nating to romance fans is that he is in many respects both the pinnacle and the antithesis of romance heroism. When I asked Bujold to tell me about Miles and his development as a hero, she said that romance heroism wasn't her focus at all: "I did not set out to create a romantic hero with Miles; I set out to create a romantic hero with Miles's dad.

"Aral Vorkosigan is pretty literally the alpha-and-omega male lead of my series (which, at the time Cordelia first rolled over to find his boots in the mud in front of her nose, on page two of My First Novel, I did not yet envision). The whole universe was built starting from him (and Cordelia) and moving outward. You can't get much more angsty-alpha-male than Viceroy Prime Minister Regent Admiral Count Aral Vorkosigan. And he has his fans, fanning themselves, as well, but his romance was a tale that I could only tell once, that being the inherent nature of such things. So when Miles came along, that niche was already explored and occupied, so to speak.

"Miles began in proto-form as something to do to his parents; I knew even before I'd finished *Shards of Honor* that their male heir would be born both bright and disabled, although I did not yet know how…

"Miles was built in part in reaction to Aral, and in part in reaction to standard genre tropes. Tall and handsome? No, short and odd. An orphan, preferably tragic, unencumbered by relations? No, plagued with scads of same—well, perhaps not scads, but they made up in density whatever they lacked in numbers. Spockian and unemotional? Nope. Passionately emotional. Unconscious of heroic ambition? Hell, no—ambitious as the devil, and wildly self-conscious in a very postmodern way. And, of course, desperate to live up to his dad's example in all ways, including the romantic. (To Miles, this of course meant Aral's marriage to Cordelia. Fortunately for Miles's peace of mind, he was largely unappraised of the more lurid details of Aral's speckled past.) I set Miles in motion on the wall, and all else followed.

"The 'bright' part stuck, because I am a geek girl—I was a geek girl back in the '60s before the concept had yet been invented or the term coined, and wasn't that ever an uncomfortable time—and intelligence is the one absolutely nonnegotiable requirement not only in a romantic hero, but in most SF protagonists of any sort.

"Miles has both positive qualities and interesting flaws. Among the former are intelligence, loyalty, a loving heart, and a quixotic passion for justice. Among the latter are hyperactivity, mood swings, a trust in his own judgment and mistrust of most other people's bordering on arrogance (we won't say which side), and a quixotic passion for adventure—or at least, he's a noted adrenaline junkie. Hard to say which set of aspects get him into the most trouble.

"Miles never really falls out of love with any woman he falls in love with, which led to a rather complex accumulation over his ensuing volumes. As one character points out, it's not that Miles picks up so many women; it's that he never puts any down. Miles [also] has high social status, wealth, and a really big house. All major romance attractors, by all the evidence. Especially the house."

You could write an entire book on heroism based on Miles alone, I think: a hero that has many, many fans among science fiction and romance readers alike, who is wealthy, titled, surrounded by intense family, and exceptionally short and scarred while the standard of beauty in his world is to be tall and flawless. On the outside, Miles is the opposite of the heroic archetype; inside, he is the quintessential hero, particularly due to his capacity to care for others. As Bujold puts it, "One must also reflect on the possibility that the standard model for a romance hero is just plain wrong, or at least mistaken in what is essential..."

Author Darlene Marshall sees Miles, his father Aral, and the other characters in Bujold's series similarly: "They're human and they make mistakes, but they rise to the occasion and most of the time act with honor, integrity, and a deep and wide ocean of caring for the people around them."

That is some heroism right there.

ROARKE

The In Death series

By J. D. Robb/Nora Roberts

Roarke is one half of a couple whose slowly developing relationship has spanned over forty books in the In Death series by Nora Roberts, writing as J. D. Robb. Roarke is an enigma: a ridiculously wealthy man with power and far-reaching influence, Roarke has lived on both sides of the law, which makes his relationship with detective Eve Dallas very tricky at times. Both Eve and Roarke have a tortured backstory that is revealed in tiny bits with each successive book, and Roarke's determination to care for the exceptionally prickly and independent Eve has created quite a following among romance fans.

Readers adore Roarke. As Nina-Mary writes, "What woman doesn't want a man who accepts her as she is, and confronts and understands her demons." R.J. says that "If Roarke only did one thing to make me love him, it would be how he holds Eve after she has a nightmare. Eve will take solace in his arms for just the bare minimum of time, until she is just barely under control, and then she pulls away. But Roarke doesn't let her go! He continues to hold on to Eve until she is calm, but also until he himself is calm. He absolutely, 100 percent needs Eve; without her, he is empty."

R.J. also points out one of Roarke's most appealing factors—he changes his life and his motivations because of Eve: "Roarke also makes a similar transformation from being the big man on the opposite side of the law from his love to helping his love who stands firmly on and for the law. The reformed man is seductive, but only when the man makes the choice to change for his love, not when the partner works so hard to change him. The change is possible when the love he has for his partner is stronger than the desire to thieve, when he loves her/him more than he loves his previous life."

What is noteworthy about Roarke and also Miles Vorkosigan is that they are heroes in ongoing series with each book culminating with a "happy-for-now" ending, not a "happily-ever-after." The investment on the part of the reader in the slow growth and character development over what could be a few years' worth of books is definitely true to life in many respects.

DAVY DEMPSEY AND PHIN
Faking It and *Welcome to Temptation*
By Jennifer Crusie

Crusie writes great dialogue, and with it men who are smart, confused by women, and yet not eager to embrace any of the stereotypical portrayals of baffled, clueless men. Davy is a con artist, or, as J. B. Hunt says on the website, "a con artist with a heart of gold. Life would never be boring with Davy." Rudi also likes Davy, in part because she likes the reformed/reforming bad boy, but also because, "I have learnt from my reading that I never really like or trust the bad boy who starts reforming because he's in love with the girl. He needs to have already taken steps for himself, by himself. Otherwise it seems kind of false and I doubt that it will stick."

Phin, the mayor of Temptation, Ohio, is caught between the heroine, Sophie, who is filming a rather impressive racy movie in his town, and the town council, who will pass any ordinance to put a stop to the spicy filmmaking. A reader who goes by Brussel Sprout says that she loves Phin because he's "witty and observant and resistant and hot, hot, hot. The heroes I love best are observant and powerful. And they have to have integrity. They can make mistakes and cock it up, but deep down, they have to be true to themselves."

Part of the charm of Crusie's heroes, particularly these two, is that they are befuddled and bothered by their emotions and have to navigate that confusion. Crusie's heroes narrate some of their own stories, so the reader learns about the heroine and the hero in equal measure.

DAIN

Lord of Scoundrels
By Loretta Chase

Lord of Scoundrels is, as you may have already read, a book used by many of us romance readers to change the minds of those who sniff disdainfully at the genre but are still curious about it enough to try one. Dain, the hero, is a complete nightmare as a person until he meets Jessica, the heroine. As reader Jay puts it, "His snarling self-sufficiency starts to melt at his first contact with Jessica, and despite all of his blustering denial, he is clearly captivated. Watching him realize it and struggle to regain his equilibrium is so satisfying. It is the story of his journey to becoming the hero worthy of Jess's strength and love."

Among the leaders of the Dain Fangirl Club is Candy, the cofounder of *Smart Bitches*, who loves this book in a million different exclamation-point-strewn ways. When I asked her why she liked Dain so much, she said, "Dain works so well for me because the book opens with his awful childhood. Most heroes with massive asshole streaks (I know that phrase can be read in a completely different way than I meant it, but I'm totally leaving that in there because it makes me laugh) spring from the pages fully-formed, like Minerva from Zeus's head, except with bigger cocks and more forceful kissing proclivities. But we get to see Dain when he was young and squishy and vulnerable. Proto-Dain isn't an asshole. Proto-Dain sought love and approval and affection. Adult Dain is what he is because Proto-Dain's gentler impulses were hammered out of him.

"I also love Dain because while he's a massive jerk, he has principles and boundaries…Dain grew into a sensitive man who ultimately had too much empathy and humanity to step over the line into brutality, which so many other romance heroes have.

"Speaking of sensitivity: another reason why I love Dain so much is that Chase quite clearly shows us, without ever telling us, that Dain is really high-strung underneath his fearsome exterior. When Jessica bothers him and his brain becomes totally disordered and he becomes borderline obsessive, or when he's confronted by his illegitimate child and all he wants is to get him away as fast as he can? If Dain could see a shrink today, the shrink would probably diagnose him with an anxiety disorder and coax him through some cognitive behavioral therapy. Dain's growth is much more believable and organic because Jessica also behaves convincingly: she consistently confronts him with his irrationality and holds him accountable for his bad behavior, and best of all, Dain eventually learns.

"And last, but not least, I love Dain because he has a sense of humor, and because he's funny without necessarily meaning to be. His personal dictionary, for example, in which he categorizes and defines various classes of people? Funny as hell. And the whip-smart, whip-quick banter between him and Jessica still stands as some of my favorite examples of dialogue in any romance novel, ever. Also, while Dain is arrogant, he isn't self-important and he doesn't take himself too seriously, which is a refreshing change from other romance heroes, because I think a lot of asshole heroes, especially those from the '70s, '80s, and early '90s, are arrogant because they're self-important twats."

He heard a rustle of movement and a muffled sound somewhere ahead and to his left. His gaze shifted thither. The female whose murmurs he'd heard was bent over a display case of jewelry. The shop was exceedingly ill lit—on purpose, to increase customers' difficulty in properly evaluating what they were looking at. All Dain could ascertain was that the female wore a blue overgarment of some sort and one of the hideously overdecorated bonnets currently in fashion.

"I particularly recommend," he went on, his eyes upon the female, "that you resist the temptation to count if you are contemplating a gift for your *chère amie*. Women deal in a higher mathematical realm than men, especially when it comes to gifts."

"That...is a consequence of the feminine brain having reached a more advanced state of development," said the female without looking up. "She recognizes that the selection of a gift requires the balancing of a profoundly complicated moral, psychological, aesthetic, and sentimental equation. I should not recommend that a mere male attempt to involve himself in the delicate process of balancing it, especially by the primitive method of counting."

For one unsettling moment, it seemed to Lord Dain that someone had just shoved his head into a privy. His heart began to pound, and his skin broke out in clammy gooseflesh...

He told himself that his breakfast had not agreed with him. The butter must have been rancid.

It was utterly unthinkable that the contemptuous feminine retort had overset him.

—*LORD OF SCOUNDRELS* BY LORETTA CHASE, 1995

DOMINIC (ALSO DOMINIC'S FATHER, THE DUKE OF AVON)
Devil's Cub
By Georgette Heyer

Dominic Alastair, called "Vidal" throughout most of *Devil's Cub*, is, to put it frankly, a complete jerkwad. He takes advantage of women, he is rather insatiable in his appetites for things he shouldn't be doing, and he thinks he is irresistible, which is why it is unabashed fun when he meets his match in Mary, the heroine.

Ros says that she "loves the bad boys who turn (almost) good once they find the right woman: Dominic Alastair (*Devil's Cub*) and Jasper Damerel (*Venetia*) are my absolute all-time favorites. Both of them are fun, clever, surprisingly caring, and utterly drop-dead gorgeous."

Broke Baroque agrees: "I tend to gravitate toward the Bad Boy end of the hero spectrum. I love me some rakes and libertines, the more dissipated and jaded the better, who are reformed by love. Well, not totally reformed, I guess—more like they fall in love and start to understand that there's more to life than getting drunk all the time. I just like the fantasy of the playboy rake turning respectable for the love of a good woman."

Alex echoes Broke's comments and says Dominic is one of her earliest ideal heroes: "I read *Devil's Cub* at a clearly impressionable age and Dominic is, and always has been, at the top of my list. Entirely Alpha but I think Heyer puts it beautifully when Mary says, 'I could manage him.' I think that one simple line sums it up, really—we want to think that we can tame a bad boy."

FREDDY
Cotillion
By Georgette Heyer

Heyer has crafted several heroes that readers adore, and Freddy is definitely one. Scribblerkat says that she adores Freddy because she loves "the Sidekicks and the Unlikely Heroes. But most of all I love the heroes whose primary characteristics are intelligence and a sense of humor. A prime example of the latter is Freddy from Georgette Heyer's *Cotillion*."

Kitzie says that "there's only one strictly romance hero that I like that would also be good in real life: Freddy from *Cotillion*. He would stand by you and make you laugh. That's way more dreamy than a muscular torso."

..... 💜 .....

And the top two heroes, the two that make the most readers swoon and make the patented Good Romance Novel Noise:

JAMIE FRASER
Outlander
By Diana Gabaldon

- AND -

FITZWILLIAM DARCY
Pride and Prejudice
By Jane Austen

Why these two? Samantha explains Fraser's appeal best: "If I were going to use a fictional character as a measuring stick for future relationships, Jamie Fraser would be it. Gabaldon doesn't gloss over his flaws. He's not a perfect specimen of humanity, physically or in his personality. [His relationship with Claire] has its ups and downs, but the bond is deeper than 'they're the hero and the heroine, and therefore they shall live happily ever after according to the laws heretofore set forth by the romance gods.'"

As for Darcy, his appeal as a romantic hero has been sustained for nearly two hundred years, since *Pride and Prejudice* was published in 1813. Part of his appeal lies in his transformation, from sullen, unyielding snob to dedicated, quiet suitor for Elizabeth Bennet's affections. Darcy initiates such a complete change to his character, all in an effort to be worthy of someone else, and that effort has earned him many a sigh-worthy moment from romance readers.

Colin Firth wet and almost-shirtless helps considerably as well.

THE TOP NINE ROMANCE HEROES

9. Miles Vorkosigan, the Vorkosigan Saga, by Lois McMaster Bujold

8. Roarke, the In Death series, by J. D. Robb

7. Davy Dempsey, *Faking It*, by Jennifer Crusie

6. Phin, *Welcome to Temptation*, by Jennifer Crusie

5. Dain, *Lord of Scoundrels*, by Loretta Chase

4. Dominic, *Devil's Cub*, by Georgette Heyer

3. Freddy, *Cotillion*, by Georgette Heyer

2. Jamie Fraser, *Outlander*, by Diana Gabaldon

1. Fitzwilliam Darcy, *Pride and Prejudice*, by Jane Austen

We Know What Not to Want

.... ♥ ....

In addition to recognizing quality people and solid relationships that can survive anything that life—or a romance author—can come up with, one of the most important codes that romance novels hide within the genre is the ability to identify what makes for damaging, hurtful, and dangerous relationships. Many romance characters are recovering from difficult or even deadly relationships with people who were abusive, sneaky, or just neglectful. From a narration standpoint, it makes for easy contrast with the hero: the hero is light years more hot, stable, kind, honorable, and worthy than the Bad Ex or the Former Husband or even the Vengeful and Somewhat Batshit-Crazy Father Figure. From a reader's standpoint, it's a laundry list of behavior to avoid and, more importantly, to recognize. What's interesting is how many romance readers recognize traits they love in fiction and in heroes which they would abhor in actual people—and how these readers can absolutely identify the differences and similarities in their own lives.

A reader on my site who goes by the name "readingin-public" says that she's noticed when something that's alluring in fiction is not at all appealing in real life: "What I love in book heroes is very off-putting in a real-life man. There's a guy in my life right now who is completely chasing me. He's very jealous, aggressive, emotionally dependent, and is a black belt in tae kwon do. But although I like the protective part, everything else is just scary, considering that he won't take NO for an answer!

"I admire that in book heroes, but the slight obsessiveness is frightening in real life. It's weird. What I read about in books, I will not always like in an actual man. I think that what I'd like in a man in real life is more the type who is willing to be pursued rather than doing the pursuing. He's got to be independent. No whining about how he can't live without me."

The romance version of the driven man who pursues the person he is interested in comes with the Romance Novel Guarantee that, by virtue of being the hero of a romance novel, this hero comes with the best and most virtuous of intentions and is meant to be with the heroine. In other words, he won't go all psychopants in the end and turn into a complete assnugget. One hopes that the author will write a convincing story that will explain or mitigate some of the driven obsessive pursuit that, as readinginpublic says, is rather alarming in real life. Someone who is "jealous, aggressive, emotionally dependent" and possessing the capability to do violence is not a benevolent protector.

It can be difficult to tell the difference between someone who has the capacity to change, and someone who is plain, unfiltered crazysauce in fiction and in real life. As Hezabelle wrote, "I like them best when they *seem* like stubborn jerks but then have this secret caring/protective side. Sadly, I like them like that in real life too. But without inner dialogue it's a lot harder to tell whether they're secretly caring or just plain stubborn jerks."

Alpha Lyra has a list of hero traits from romances she cannot stand that apply to both real and fictional men: "Rakes (all I can think of is how many STDs they must have). Asshats. Passive men lacking in ambition or passion. Misogynists (men who hate all women until they meet the heroine)."

If you're not familiar with the term, "rake" refers to a male who has an absolutely jaw-dropping number of sexual partners in his back story and is, in short, a giant slut with a coating of titanium to keep the diseases away. Rakes hold a certain appeal for some readers, but only in fiction, probably because of that mythical titanium shield! Kitzie says that "My favorite heroes are mostly rakes. I think they are vulnerable but strong, able to find a way to avoid hurt, even if it's not the best road to happiness. The best are Sebastian from *Devil in Winter* (Evie sees through to his sensitive parts, and he loves her anyway) and Vidal in *Devil's Cub* (when he actually acts his age and begs his father to tell Mary she must marry him? I just die. Plus, Mary shoots him. 'Nuf said). But a rake wouldn't do in real life—they never deal well with people seeing past their facades."

His self-control, always so solid, evaporated like hot water on a stove plate. "I'm not worried about you, damn it! It's just—holy hell, it's not done, Evie. The Viscountess St. Vincent can't live in a gaming club, even for a few days."

"I didn't realize you were so conventional," she said, and for some reason the sight of his ferocious scowl elicited a twitch of amusement at the corners of her lips. As subtle as the twitch was, Sebastian saw it, and he was instantly thrown from anger to bemusement. He would be damned if he would be put through a wringer by a twenty-three-year-old virgin...near-virgin...who was so naïve as to believe that she was any kind of match for him."

—*DEVIL IN WINTER* BY LISA KLEYPAS, 2006

A reader named Wendy says, "Seriously. I love me some brooding, Possible Interesting Secret Damage in a book, but in life: yikes. No.

"My real-life this–does–not–work example: My sister keeps dating these lovely musicians who come off either mysterious or playful (with a hidden something), but to a man, they live with their parents in their mid to late twenties. Under the smoldering, reading of philosophy, and talent, the immaturity is *VAST*. She's care-taking, and they may or may not pick up the ball when she needs them to. I understand the attraction, but no. I want a guy who will drive me to work when the roads are icy and wash the dishes—partnership and small care-taking—and still think that spontaneous sexoring on the stairs is a really good idea."

Sometimes, finding a man who in one key way is the opposite of a preferred type can make a huge difference, as Joanna S. explains: "The types of dominant men/heroes who make me tingle deliciously in my no-no place in romance novels would make me run screaming in real life, or possibly dial 911 upon meeting them. The good news is that I did finally find my Stoic Alpha in real life, and I knew he was my dream guy when, three months into our relationship, I asked how he felt about me, and he looked me dead in the eye and said (without any hesitation or stammering), 'I love you, of course!!' Mrowr."

Sallie decided that, after reading about too many, "damaged, brooding, tormented heroes really aren't attractive. There's no strength or desire in me to engage their demons; I have my own.

"I passed on a romance with a troubled man in favor of one with my husband, a transparent, peaceable, optimistic man who had a happy childhood. The odd thing is, my husband *does* find damaged, hurt women attractive. He wants to fix them and make them happy, which was my good luck. But since I do not find anger, depression, and pain attractive, and I know they're not good for children, I give my family the best of me that I can.

"This is what romance novels never, never told me, but life has: it is fantasy—foolishness if you expect it in life—to think that you can be the heroine who tames the alpha rake and turns him into a devoted, faithful husband, all for the love of you. It is much more sensible to start off with the nice guy who loves you and wants to be true."

Without the "Romance Novel Guarantee"™ and its assurance of the happily-ever-after by page three-hundred-whatever, it can be difficult to see past the negatives, especially without any signal that there are heroic qualities as well. Tracy Hopkins says that she is "also attracted to the fictional kinds of guys that sensible me would never go for in real life: J. R. Ward's Zsadist as the damaged soul screams for me…but in real life? Too much baggage. In a romance novel, you know the guy is going to turn out okay, so it's OK to love him…in sensible real life, you *know* you're never going to fix him so you need to *stay away*. In real life, I've been known to try, unfortunately.

"Stan from Suzanne Brockmann's *Over the Edge* is one I go for in fiction *and* in real life…the protector sort. My real-life protector doesn't have abs that nice, though. On the other hand, he's real. And sensible."

Laurel similarly has a line between real-life-possibility and no-freaking-way when it comes to hero behavior: "I like some Alpha in my heroes, borderline overbearing, but never, ever, ever disrespectful. It's a tricky balance between slightly overprotective and 'don't you worry your pretty little head, sugar britches.'"

Milena agrees: "I, too, often like heroes who would not be charming in real life. There's one important thing for heroes to work for me both in books and in real life, and that's understanding that they were wrong and trying to make it right.

One of the latest examples that comes to mind is Rhys from *Iron Duke*: he's obnoxious at first, but slowly learns how not to be—and that's when his best qualities really get to shine."

"I like some Alpha in my heroes, borderline overbearing, but never, ever, ever disrespectful. It's a tricky balance between slightly overprotective and 'don't you worry your pretty little head, sugar britches.'"—LAUREL, A READER

AThrillingYarn explains why romance readers adore certain heroes—and what reading about the heroic perfection in some fictional novels gives to readers: "The hero is not perfect for every or any woman out there; he is perfect for that specific heroine. I think it makes the reader have more hope for her own life or relationship. Not every girl will be able to land a Brad Pitt or a Fabio, but you have a realistic chance at that one man who is flawed, but flawed in a way that you can stand, and maybe even complement. Freddy in [Georgette Heyer's] *Cotillion* is wonderful because he does small things and isn't the most handsome or the most intelligent or the most charming, but he is the RIGHT man and the man that will make THAT heroine happiest. *The Grand Sophy* has another great hero that would be a horrible match for many ladies, but is perfect for

Sophy. There isn't much to the book after the proposal, but you close the pages knowing that they will bring out the best in each other for the entire marriage."

Caitlin, as well, learned from older romances what she definitely Did Not Want in a hero: "They taught me what type of future partner I wanted. In my early forays into romance, it was one of the few book types not commonly in the house. So the stuff I picked up was from car boot sales and fairly old, and the heroes were such DICKS. They were strong, and passionate, and mentally and physically steadfast, which I learned I liked, but they were SO HORRIBLE. Why couldn't they just talk about things? Why couldn't they just say they loved her? So subconsciously I resolved to find a partner with their good traits, while simultaneously actively deciding to find someone who wasn't a complete TOSSPOT.

....

"The hero is not perfect for every or any woman out there; he is perfect for that specific heroine. I think it makes the reader have more hope for her own life or own relationship... You close the pages knowing that they will bring out the best in each other for the entire marriage."—ATHRILLINGYARN, A READER

....

"Later, romances taught me not to settle. Young women are frequently taught to settle. With their high-school boyfriend, or anyone who is 'good enough.' Not to say there is any such thing as a perfect person, as a soul mate, just two people with a lot in common who love each other—romance novels trained me into thinking I was worthy of adoration, not just someone who kept me around, thought I was cute, and guessed they could put up with me. Someone who saw every part of me and loved me so fiercely it was insane. Someone who loved me, in short, like a romance novel hero. And I was told that sort of love doesn't exist, that it doesn't stand up to every day, that men are borderline dumb animals who have to be trained into humanity. But I looked, because I wouldn't settle. I couldn't imagine anything more soul-destroying, and after a lot of fun, I found someone exactly like that. And that romance-novel love has lasted seven years, through severe illnesses, depression, his terrible farts, etc. As I said to him, if you can both have the norovirus at the same time (Google it) and still look at each other three days later and love each other and want to jump each other's bones, three days after you were too scared to fart in case it wasn't a fart, you know it's real."

By far my favorite comment from all the authors and readers who responded to my questions and requests for help came from Robyn Carr, who looked at the idea of what readers and writers learned from romance, and how happy-ever-afters can be taught one book at a time, and turned that question on its head: "I think the antithesis of the question is more important—what do we learn from romance novels that we shouldn't get over?

....

"Romance novels trained me into thinking I was worthy of adoration, not just someone who kept me around, thought I was cute, and guessed they could put up with me. Someone who saw every part of me and loved me so fiercely it was insane. Someone who loved me, in short, like a romance novel hero."—CAITLIN, A READER

....

"When our heroines walk away from lying, cheating, abusive relationships, our readers stand up and cheer! When our heroes fail to fall for mean, selfish, manipulative women, our readers applaud! Men and women in real life and in romance novels find themselves trapped in unhealthy, destructive relationships all the time, and when they choose to believe they deserve love, respect, and healthy, enduring relationships, when they reclaim their lives and demand only excellent treatment and a love they can fully trust, life is good. Readers are not only satisfied—they use those characters as role models."

We Know How to Spot
Real-Life Heroes and Heroines

I f you watch television at all, or have perhaps flipped through a popular magazine in the last few years, you might have noticed that it's kind of hard (ha!) to be a guy right now. The male beauty industry has made some serious strides in potentially high-cost product marketing. There are new male body colognes, body washes, hair dyes, skin care products—all with that same condescending tone that women receive from the beauty industry as well. To wit: "You do not look good right now. We might be able to help." Both genders are told regularly they aren't thin, bulky, hairless, hairy, svelte, muscular, or perfect enough. And it's easy to arrive at the conclusion that romance novels propagate the idea that the pinnacle of beauty is a level to which most humans cannot ascend, and that therefore most folks can't be romance heroes or heroines.

So not true. I'll tell you why.

Each gender is schooled in a standard of beauty and we're programmed to notice when others of the same gender do not live up to that standard. But when it comes to the objects of our affection, regardless of their gender, we don't notice any of that stuff. Ordinary people are way more heroic than the airbrushed super-enhanced image of any model, anywhere (even in the shower, or on a horse, with or without Old Spice).

The real heroic traits for men and for women are much trickier to sustain in real life than keeping a perfect mullet all mullety with gleaming mulletness. Moreover, they are all internal characteristics and things you likely learned as a child when you were taught how to treat other people (the difference now being that biting other people, when consensual, is much more acceptable). So what are the traits that form the foundation of a hero or heroine? Funny you should ask, because romance authors and readers know them all—particularly Loretta Chase, who, as I said earlier, pretty much knows everything, including tomorrow's lottery numbers.

TRAITS OF AN IDEAL ROMANCE CHARACTER*

- respect
- honesty
- compassion
- honor

- courage
- intelligence
- sense of humor

*Also, the traits of a decent human being—quelle surprise!

New York Times bestselling author Robyn Carr says that **RESPECT** is the key ingredient in a hero or heroine: "It supersedes all. It doesn't mean they never quarrel or misunderstand or get angry—but it means fighting fair, striving to understand, and [having] a willingness to forgive. Men and women in life and in romance should have basic, fundamental respect for their opposite sex; for all human beings, for that matter. And, when some action or behavior causes a loss of respect and trust, that happily-ever-after cannot come into focus until it's restored."

New York Times bestselling author Jennifer Crusie, author of *Bet Me*, one of my favorite contemporary romances, says that one of the most important elements to being a hero is **COMPASSION**, but that not every romance hero is a one-size-fits-all parallel to humanity: "I don't believe in romance rules. But for me, a big one is empathy, that ability to understand the other person's experience. Another one is respect for others, a sort of global application of the old idea of watching to see how your date treats the wait staff.

"I think a character has to be complete in herself or himself before she or he can emotionally connect to another in a partnership. The old 'you complete me' line makes my blood run cold. If they have all of that going for them, then they're likely not to lie or cheat or stalk or do any of the other things that kneecap a relationship."

Anna Campbell, another *New York Times* bestselling author (I think I'm going to be writing that phrase a lot in this book), echoed Crusie's sentiments on empathy: "You know, the fun answer to this would be a big, powerful chest and bulging biceps and a lantern jaw and a lot of (ahem!) stamina. And that's just the heroine! But the real (and less fun) answer is all the old golden virtues—you know, **HONESTY AND COURAGE AND INTELLIGENCE AND KINDNESS AND HONOR AND A SENSE OF HUMOR**. An ability to forgive comes in handy. Empathy for another person's suffering. Self-sacrifice for the beloved. Sometimes our hero and heroine start out with all this good stuff. Sometimes they have to learn it."

"You've got to find your own way, your own answers." Ray smiled at Ethan out of brilliantly blue eyes, and Ethan could see the creases deepen around them. "It means more that way. I'm proud of you."

Ethan felt his throat burn, his heart squeeze. Routinely he rebaited the pot, then watched the orange floats bob on the water. "For what?"

"For being. Just for being Ethan."

—*RISING TIDES* BY NORA ROBERTS, 1998

Nora Roberts agrees that the individual must be complete before pairing up with someone else: "I think to engage the writer's, the reader's (especially if it's me), and the romantic partner's respect, a hero or heroine must have—and this is a quote from Mary Blayney—'honor at the core.' Whatever they've done or will do, no matter how flawed they are, there has to be that **CENTRAL CORE OF HONOR**.

"They must be open, or learn to be open, to love, to compromise, and please God to humor. If they're closed off, and remain so, they're likely going to be too stubborn, selfish, humorless, and egotistical to engage my interest as a writer and as a reader…

"If the hero or heroine is a complete asshole, if he or she is physically or emotionally abusive, lacks that core of honor, I'm not going to care enough about them to read their story. Unless they develop that core, unless they evolve, grow during the course of the story. That may very well be the point of the story, and could be brilliantly done. Love changes the asshole."

Jill Shalvis says, "I always like to say that heroes (and heroines) can look, talk, and act differently but the one trait they have to possess is **A GOOD HEART**. It's a requirement."

She'd been working for Wilder Adventures for a week now, the best week in recent memory. Up until right this second when a shadowy outline of a man appeared in her room. Like the newly brave woman she was, she threw the covers over her head and hoped he hadn't seen her.

"Hey," he said, blowing that hope all to hell.

His voice was low and husky, sounding just as

surprised as she. With a deep breath, she lurched upright to a seated position on the bed and reached out for her handy-dandy baseball bat before remembering she hadn't brought it with her. Instead, her hands connected with her glasses and they went flying.

Which might just have been a blessing in disguise, because now she wouldn't be able to witness her own death.

But then the tall shadow bent and scooped up her glasses and...

Handed them to her.

A considerate bad guy?

—*INSTANT ATTRACTION* BY JILL SHALVIS, 2009

Author Sarah MacLean holds her heroes to the same standards as her heroines—and on both sides of the heroic equation there is plenty of work and behavior to emulate: "Even though I write historicals, in which many seem to expect that relationships be inherently unequal because of the time period, I say we shouldn't expect anything more of our heroes than we do our heroines. And vice versa. Great relationships are based on equality. So here are my requirements for heroes, heroines, and happily-ever-afters:

1. Don't be mean.
2. Don't cheat.

3. If you hurt the person you love, apologize (if groveling is necessary—and it probably is—don't phone it in).

4. And finally and most importantly, trust your partner. Trust, trust, trust. Far too many romances (in both real life and in romancelandia) brush over this one. I don't understand relationships that rely on shared email accounts or (worse) account hacking. I don't understand relationships that require hourly check-ins by phone or text. And I definitely don't understand romance heroes who lose their jealous minds when they see their obviously loving heroines talking to other men. It's not sexy. It's scary.

"Let me say it again. **TRUST** your partner. If you can't, this is probably not going to work."

Author Alexis Harrington has a working model for creating a romance hero: "A hero doesn't need to be perfect— I'd rather have a man with human frailties and self-doubts. But despite his imperfections, he must have a **NOBILITY OF SPIRIT** that gives him the ability to recognize his own flaws, to see the good in others, and ultimately, to do the right thing, regardless of the cost to himself."

Eloisa James, *New York Times* bestselling author of more than eighteen novels, points out that the courtship isn't always the most difficult or emotionally challenging part of a relationship: "I think marriage is really tough—it's one of the reasons that I don't write romances that end at the altar. And very often people need to learn those rules of conduct while married, rather than before. So I think that partners need to be thoughtful, empathetic (i.e., able to imagine what the other person is thinking), sensuous (interested in pleasure—the frequency or athleticism of the event is not important), and loving. The last is probably most important. It's actually not all that easy to learn to be loving—to take care of the other person, to think of them, to love them. It's a lot easier to get irritated. So I'll add patience. I certainly have learned a lot about patience as a married person.

"Finally, you have to be **FAITHFUL**. Unfaithfulness—emotional or physical—destroys a relationship." And that's true in or out of a romance novel—but you knew that, right? Of course you did."

Teresa Medeiros has very specific ideas about the rules of conduct for a hero or heroine, and she defines the lines they absolutely cannot cross—lines that work both in fiction and in reality:

1. A romance hero or heroine might end up in a battle of wit and wills with their partner but they would never ever emotionally demean or physically abuse them.
2. They're more likely to find the beauty in their partner that the rest of the world may have missed.
3. They're also faithful. From the first moment their gazes meet, they don't have eyes for anyone else.
4. And a romance heroine doesn't just stand by her man. She stands up to him! And he adores and respects her even more for having the courage to do so.
5. A romance hero must always be willing to rush into a burning building to save a basket of kittens.

Christina Dodd says that romance protagonists can get away with doing just about anything so long as there's a good reason: heroes and heroines "get to have a different code of conduct than the rest of us, i.e., they can do crummy things as long as they do them for an honorable cause.

"For instance, in *The Barefoot Princess*, an historical romance, Princess Amy kidnaps Jermyn Edmondson, marquess of Northcliff, and chains him in her basement because she believes he had destroyed the livelihood of her village (and because he was the lord of the land and he'd thoughtlessly turned over the stewardship to his wicked uncle, he was ultimately responsible). The action is reprehensible. The reason is honorable. It's a simple plan, destined to succeed—except that Uncle Harrison is Jermyn's heir and he would be delighted if someone killed his nephew and left him with the title and fortune, and Jermyn is handsome, arrogant, and a little cranky with Amy for manacling him."

Kresley Cole says that to construct the ideal hero and heroine, the trust and respect are obvious and required, but "they also need **A SHARED SENSE OF HUMOR** to have a chance at a lasting HEA. I believe humor is a buffer against the everyday aggravations that can wear on a relationship. If I read a scene with the hero and heroine laughing together, then I feel much more confident about their HEA."

Suddenly, she twirled around and brushed a sizzling kiss on his cheek. His eyes narrowed suspiciously at her, but she merely laughed. "It's called—say it with me—a-fec-shun."

He'd just assumed she flirted because that was her nature. Yet could she...could she truly be interested in him? Even attracted to him—with his red eyes and scars?...

"Why would you show me affection?"

She answered, "Because I...feel it?"

"Why?"

With a laugh, she asked, "Why, why, why? Must you question everything good?"

—*DARK NEEDS AT NIGHT'S EDGE*
BY KRESLEY COLE, 2008

Author Rachel Gibson says that reality is the major draw for readers and writers, because her characters have to seem possible: "For me personally, the hero and heroine must seem like real people. Real people with real problems who handle them realistically.

"In order for a hero and heroine to earn their happy-ever-after, they have to learn and grow as people. They have to start at one place and grow as human beings. The growth can be as simple as forgiveness or as complicated as overcoming death or betrayal. I believe that fiction has to be even more realistic than real life."

Grace Draven agrees, and says her own ideal hero and heroine wish list helped her create the hero and heroine of her book *Master of Crows*. She combined a terribly grumpy and flawed hero with an inner core of honor and integrity, and a shy, plain heroine with a tremendous personal strength. Martise of Asher bargains with her masters for her freedom: she will spy on a feared sorcerer, Silhara of Neith, and find enough evidence of wrongdoing that her masters can get rid of him. But when she falls in love with him, she learns that he is corrupted—literally. An evil god has invaded Silhara's consciousness, tempting him with limitless power if Silhara will help this god rule over the world. According to Draven, the best romance heroes and heroines display "the commonality of **HUMANITY** in all its dirty glory, with a spit-shine of heroism to make it respectable."

Honesty and the ability to deal with real human emotions is a major element that author Caridad Ferrer uses to develop her heroes, who, because Ferrer writes young adult romance, are younger than the usual romance hero: "The thing about love is that it's scary and we see it over and over in the books we love, how it prompts people to behave in crazy ways that are driven by the fear that sort of intense emotion tends to provoke. So it's not just about being honest with each other—characters need to be **HONEST WITH THEMSELVES** and have that pep talk and go, hey, you know, this love stuff? It's terrifying."

Reader Darlynne encompasses all true heroic traits when she says that "in real life and fiction, and after thirty-four years of marriage, the most enduring, endearing, and important characteristics of a hero for me are these: Is he someone to be trusted with all the things that matter? Does this person have the respect of his peers? Is he someone others count on?

"The fictional hero-type that fits this bill for me is Cosmo Richter from Suzanne Brockmann's *Hot Target*. He is equal to all situations except the emotional ones. He has a plan, a course of action; he is prepared and ready. People count on him and know their lives are safe in his hands.

"In one word: **CAPABLE**. And **CONSTANT**. Okay, that's two words. Make it three: **HONORABLE**.

"My husband is all this. And you can quote me on that."

Dee says, "I think that the main traits that I adore in my heroes are that they don't necessarily see the flaws but the great things the female protagonist offers. He sees her as the epitome of beauty no matter what society's variation of beauty is at that moment. It's not that he loves her because she's flawless, but he loves her because those 'flaws' make her who she is."

Orangehands echoes that the focus on the attraction and not the standard of beauty is affirming to her as well: "Physical attraction is usually important, but physical beauty is not. I don't like it when the hero falls in love because of beauty. I want the heroes to love the heroines for a core part of their personalities. For instance, the reason Rupert from *Mr. Impossible* by Loretta Chase is my favorite historical romance hero is because of how he loves Daphne's intelligence. (And Daphne is one of my favorites because she has that intelligence.) But he never once wanted her to be stupid, but rather wanted her to be as smart as she could, as she was."

Ultimately, romance novels aren't about the heroic ideal, or individuals who are so perfect, real humanity can't measure up. Certainly some portions of the novels and the characters within them are idealized, but really, the pairing of the protagonists is what matters. They are not perfect, but perfect for one another. They are made up of characteristics highlighted here that just about anyone can acquire and demonstrate—if not all, then many of them. Not being a complete douchecanoe is the first step in being your own ideal romance hero or heroine—and it's absolutely an attainable ideal.

And when ideal matches meet, many Good Things can happen.

"He never once wanted her to be stupid, but rather wanted her to be as smart as she could, as she was."—ORANGEHANDS, A READER, ON LORETTA CHASE'S *MR. IMPOSSIBLE*

We Know Good Sex

♥

Just as the average romance heroine doesn't sit around filing her nails and looking pretty, waiting for her hero to ride in and sweep her away to connubial bliss, so it is with sex. Sitting there does nothing. If you just lie there and wait for it, it won't be very satisfying.

Sex in a romance novel is a tricky subject, but let me make one thing quite clear: sex depictions in romance novels have changed drastically, and the rapetastic romances are things of the past, thank heaven and all available orgasms. In romances published today, not only is the sexuality a variable part of the plot—some books feature mere kisses, and some feature acts of kinky you might never have heard of in your life that may possibly defy laws of gravity and physics—but both parties participate in making sure the sexuality is fantastic for all involved.

I'll be frank (ha!) and get the negative out of the way first: part of the problem with romance novel sex is that it is so impossibly perfect, so incredibly over-the-top wonderful, that real sex can seem messy and awkward in comparison sometimes. This is likely because real sex is sometimes awkward and messy.

This is one thing I don't understand about pornography, and yes, I've seen some (and no, it wasn't a romance novel). Two people having sex? Weird looking. How is this attractive or alluring? Let's not kid ourselves. Sexual intercourse is not the sensuously choreographed ballet as old as time. Sometimes it is the elbows-and-ouch-you're-on-my-hair as old as time.

Yet sexuality is an enduring part of the romance genre, and one of the reasons it takes so much crap from people who don't read it or understand it. Courtship is based in part on sexual attraction, and the exploration of that sexual attraction can add to the already increasing tension between the protagonists.

But in a romance novel, sex is often more than "just sex." Sex in a romance novel is a climax of many parts. It's the physical climax of the protagonists, plus sometimes it's the emotional climax of their attraction to each other, and the pinnacle or start of many more problems for them both. Sex never solves anything in a romance novel–if anything, it makes things more complicated.

In other words, *of course* there is sex in romance. Courtship and the relationships that follow are sexual in nature!

Sex is important, too, because it is a very common expression of intimacy. One of the first determinations in many states when a couple petitions for a divorce is whether they've had sexual relations within a certain amount of time, say six months or a year, because that sex indicates intimacy that undermines the petition for a divorce. A marriage without any sex whatsoever would not necessarily be considered a healthy one by many a relationship counselor—but not because the physical act of sexual congress is itself a requirement. Denise A. Donnelly, a sociology professor at Georgia State University who studies sexless marriages, said in a recent *New York Times* interview that "there is a feedback relationship in most couples between happiness and having sex. Happy couples have more sex, and the more sex a couple has, the happier they report being."

Sexual intercourse is not the sensuously choreographed ballet as old as time. Sometimes it is the elbows-and-ouch-you're-on-my-hair as old as time.

But Donnelly points out that sexual relations are not the point. The requirement is intimacy: "Keep in mind that sex is only one form of intimacy, and that some couples are fairly happy (and intimate) even without sex." In other words, intimacy is a requirement for healthy relationships. Yet there are few options for discussing intimacy, sex, and our own sexuality openly and honestly. Sex and intimacy are very taboo topics for many, and sexual curiosity, though natural, is more often answered with Internet pornography and rumors and misinformation than with an honest conversation.

Romance novels, on the other hand, offer safe spaces of sexual exploration and, to be honest, research on what it means to be intimate. Sexuality in romances is often portrayed within the context of a relationship and between monogamous and committed individuals. Sexual depictions in romances are also mostly positive and affirming, and in most cases, there are orgasms aplenty to go around (and around and around).

So what happens when a few billion dollars are spent on romance, and many, many, many women (and some men) read about courtship and sex? Many, many good things. Sexuality and intimacy are an integral part of romance, and to quote, well, myself, reading about women and men experiencing sexual honesty along with their sexual agency is a very powerful (and subversive) thing.

Sex in a romance can be fun, silly, emotional, intense, erotic, or all of the above. The highlight of sexual intercourse with romance heroes is not just dramatic loss of virginity anymore. With the increasing popularity of erotic romance, you can experience between the book covers what you might wonder about but not quite be ready to try underneath your own covers. There's role-playing, dominance and submission games, bondage, fantasies, sex in strange and adventurous places—and with strange and adventurous people.

Reading about passionate sex and sex as a method to express emotional passion has two benefits. First, you get to think about, or mentally try out, acts that you're curious about without actually doing them—and potentially discovering that, no, you don't like ball gags or being called "mistress" but the idea of being tied up sure cranks your engine.

> You can experience between the book covers what you might... not quite be ready to try underneath your own covers.

Second, you are able to read and learn in privacy.

Let's be honest: there are not many venues through which women can learn about sex and sexuality with judgment-free and honest communication. Women's sexuality is tied up in so many frustrating power struggles throughout history that there's shame, embarrassment, and fear for many when asking honestly what sex can and should be like.

Romance heroines are usually on journeys of self-discovery, including and not excluding sexual self-discovery. Moreover, they often have to overcome feelings of ambivalence or fear when attempting to identify and describe their own sexual desires. Author Toni Blake says, "My heroines are not nearly so dangerous as my heroes, but many of them are in a struggle to fully embrace and explore their sensuality/sexuality. This has always been a big topic in my work because I feel that many women of my generation were taught to be 'good girls' and that the message becomes so deeply entrenched that it can be a lifelong label we wear both in and out of the bedroom, forcing us to stifle valid, vital parts of who we are.

"And while having sex with a stranger in the woods up against a tree (as Jenny does in the first chapter of *One Reckless Summer*) may not be advisable in real life, I feel that in fiction sometimes you need to be a little extreme to get the point across, to jar the reader a little and make her consider the possibilities, make her ask herself questions: Could I ever do this? Could I ever want to do this? Following a fictional character's journey allows women a safe way to begin thinking about situations and actions that might have, up to now, felt forbidden to them. And it allows them to see a likable, relatable woman accepting and enjoying her sexual desires, her sexual self."

...She could have stopped this—yet still she didn't. She simply stood there soaking up the heat of his body on an already hot summer night...She heard herself whimper as forbidden pleasure arced through her. Oh, God, it felt good. To be touched. Wanted. Desired. It was the first time she'd felt...truly womanly, sexual, in years.

—*ONE RECKLESS SUMMER* BY TONI BLAKE, 2009

So can that fictional journey affect the reader and the reader's real life? You bet your sweet bippy it can. Blake told me, "I get a significant amount of e-mail from women thanking me for helping them to embrace their sexuality, and hence, ultimately improving their marriages.

"One woman rode six hours on a train to meet me at a book signing, to tell me that I'd revolutionized her relationship with sex, that I'd helped her to understand that it was A-okay to think about it, and to not censor the more explicit thoughts in her mind. She realized that embracing her sexual self didn't change her life or who she was at the core, and that 'the next morning I got up, ate breakfast, and realized the world wasn't going to end just because I was thinking dirty thoughts.'"

Reader Liz echoes Blake's comments about sexual repression, and says that "reading romance novels helped me to realize that sex is not a bad thing. My mom is a bit of a prude, and as far back as I can remember she drilled into me how having sex before you're married is bad. There were times that she would point out how premarital sex 'ruined' the lives of my aunts (she lived for dramatics—sex did not ruin my aunts' lives). Even when I was in high school, she told me that the only way to be a 'good girl' was to be like St. Mary and to wait until after marriage to have sex. There were times when I had the feeling that she wanted me to be knocked up by the Holy Spirit. She has eased up a bit since I graduated high school, but there are still times when I catch her looking at me as if she is trying to gauge whether or not I am still a virgin."

Romances have set an example not of abstinence-by-threat but of abstinence-by-choice for Liz, and have encouraged her to think critically about sex: "Most of my friends were having sex way before they were ready, and while I was just as curious as they were, I feel like the books gave me a peek at what was really going on behind closed doors, so I didn't need to hook up with random guys. In a way, romance novels taught me more about smart sexual decisions than my mother ever could. Because she didn't want me experimenting, she tried very hard to stop me from reading romance novels, which she thought would make me want to have sex before I was married. If only she knew."

"Reading romance novels helped me to realize that sex is not a bad thing... In a way, romance novels taught me more about smart sexual decisions than my mother ever could."—LIZ, A READER

Author Teresa Medeiros has also received responses from readers about the sensual content of her books: "I've had friends at church tell me that their husbands would like to thank me because they're so much more receptive to 'romance' after they read my books!"

Author Christina Dodd has similar reactions from readers: "Readers thank me for enhancing their sex lives. Single women (most of my readers who admit to being my readers are female) thank me for a good solitary experience. Women in long-time relationships tell me reading about good sex rejuvenates their sex drive, that they read passages to their husbands and Good Things happen, that their husbands buy them e-readers and gift cards so they can continue to read because the guys recognize that, even without reading the books themselves, they're getting a huge benefit.

"When a reader comments that her husband is jealous or threatened by her reading, I think a couple of things: we've got a guy who's pathetically unsure of his masculinity, and we've got a relationship that is not going to succeed. And that's sad."

Dodd also says that romances have created a warming trend for her own relationship: her husband has read many of her books, and "when he reads my books, it's also great for our sex life. All men should read romances. 'Nuf said."

Author Robyn Carr was worried about the sexuality of her novels until she asked a friend to read a manuscript for her: "One of the most important things romance novels do is create a feeling of healthy desire. As long as it's not pathological (as in obsessive and unhealthy), desire is good for men and women. A long time back, when I thought the romances I was writing were getting lots sexier, I asked a good friend with decades of experience in books to have a look. She was eighty at the time and I wanted to write a sexier novel, but I didn't want to cross the line and lose earlier readers and I asked her to give me an opinion before the manuscript was turned in. She called with many comments about the book, then finally said, 'And Robyn, about that shower scene…' I thought, oh damn, I've done it; I've gone too far. But she said, 'That brought back wonderful memories.'

"She reminded me that even when our own private lives with partners aren't benefiting from our reading, sometimes those sweet memories of the romance once enjoyed can be a bonus. I know that my friend had a long, loving, and happy marriage before she lost her husband."

Steph discovered romances because her mother let her read them as an introduction to sexuality: "I started to read romance when I was around eleven or twelve. My mom gave me a couple of her books and said I might find them interesting. Boy, did I ever! When I was done she asked if I had any questions, which I of course did, and she answered every one of them. Reading romance books made it easy to talk about sex with her, what could actually happen, how a man really should treat me, and gave us something to actually talk about in my teen years instead of fighting.

....

> **"[The] sweet memories of the romance
> once enjoyed can be a bonus."**
> —ROBYN CARR

....

"Even though they are not real people and the stories are fantasy, romance novels have been great companions through the years and something I am hoping to share with my daughters."

"Through the years they have kept me company and gave me a place to hide in some very dark and lonely times in my life. After I married they also made the nights during the many months...that my husband had been deployed shorter, less scary, and helped me relax and not worry." —STEPH, A READER

Joanna Shearer's upbringing was the opposite of reader Liz's, but romance novels had the same effect: "Romance novels made me feel safe in my fantasies about sex before I was actually ready to 'do it.' My mother was a nurse, and so she and my father have a very healthy sex life (something she consistently tries to tell me about to this day no matter how much I run around screaming, 'lalalalalalalalalala,' with my ears plugged), so I always knew the dangers of sex (diseases, unplanned pregnancy, perceptions of sluttiness, etc.) and that sex with the right person is wonderful; however, apart from their teachings and example, romance novels helped me realize that, as long as I could explore sex in books, I did not have to have sex in real life no matter how much my friends talked about it or made me feel less 'mature' for not experiencing it, because I was experiencing it, just not in a way that made me uncomfortable.

....

> "Reading romance books made it easy to talk about sex with [my mom], what could actually happen, how a man really should treat me, and gave us something to actually talk about in my teen years instead of fighting." —STEPH, A READER

....

"I know my mother worried that I would have unrealistic expectations about men, relationships, and sex because she introduced me to romance novels (in her mind) too early. Let's face it, not all men are hung the way romance heroes are or can do the sexually dynamic things they do in romance novels, any more than it is possible for a real woman to orgasm fourteen times in one carriage ride as they are wont to do in the pages of the books we love.

"But my mother needn't have worried. In reality, the heroes and heroines in romance novels taught me that I could own my sexuality on my terms, that I could respect myself enough to wait to find the right person to do all the romantic and naughty things I'd ever read about, and finally, they gave me the hope to know that, no matter how many failed relationships came before, when I found the right guy it would by no means be easy, but it would be magical. I am far from being a virgin, but the lessons about waiting for the right time and finding the right one still resonate with me. And now, as I am getting married for the first time at thirty-three years of age to the love of my life, I can tell you that it was well worth the wait on both counts!"

So romance, a genre that is often mocked and maligned as being riddled with sexuality, can be seen as a means to abstinence and waiting for the right person to experience sex? Yup! Anda has a similar story: "At the time where I was reading romance novels, the heroine was always a virgin and the guy taking her virginity was always her one, true, and forever love.

"So when my first boyfriend started pressuring me for sex, I said no because I wasn't sure if he was Mr. Right (he wasn't). He lost interest, dumped me, and I ended up keeping my virginity… until I met someone to whom it really was worth losing. So yes, I did learn from romance novels to wait and hold out until I was with someone I was really sure was one of the good guys."

"[Romance novels] gave me the hope to know that, no matter how many failed relationships came before, when I found the right guy it would by no means be easy, but it would be magical."—JOANNA SHEARER, A READER

A reader who asked that she remain anonymous, so let's call her Janet Smith, says that romances helped her understand that it was absolutely acceptable for women, as Blake pointed out, to have sexual desires: "Romance novels did have an influence on my relationships, and it was mostly a positive influence. My mom was open in talking about sex with me, so I knew all about it. And I'd decided that I was going to hold on to my virginity until I was married. And mom had made it clear that it was a boyfriend's role in a relationship to push for sex and my role to say no. So you can imagine my surprise when *I* was feeling attraction. I hadn't been prepared for the idea that *I* would want sex. I muddled through that mess on my own and decided that even though I was some kind of weird sexaholic (I thought) girl, that it was OK to do it with my boyfriend, because we were going to get married.

"I was in college by then, but didn't have girlfriends who were having sex and sharing details. Then I discovered romance novels. And you know what? The women in the novels? They liked sex! They wanted it! I wasn't a sexaholic; I was probably pretty darn normal. Go figure!"

Catinbody echoes Janet's comments about discovering her own sexuality and hornypants: "Practical things aside, I think discovering your own sexuality is a healthy part of development that helps tremendously once you're in a sexual relationship. For me, reading romance was a part of that development. I remember having it very clear in my mind at fifteen that while I didn't want a man to love me for my body, I wanted to experience a man loving my body. This seemed to be a fairly subversive idea both for someone well-ensconced in her church youth group and who was growing up in an area with strong feminist influences. But it's nothing more than what we all want—to be desired and to be loved. Romance got me honest about this and down off some of the pillars of ideology (both religious and feminist) I'd been standing on."

"Mom had made it clear that it was a boyfriend's role in a relationship to push for sex and my role to say no. So you can imagine my surprise when *I* was feeling attraction. I hadn't been prepared for the idea that *I* would want sex...Then I discovered romance novels. And you know what? The women in the novels? They liked sex! They wanted it! I wasn't a sexaholic; I was probably pretty darn normal. Go figure!"—ANONYMOUS, A READER

Romance helped Nadia in many respects, especially in her marriage: "I learned a lot early on about what's good for a female, and that sex can and should be good for the female, and applied it in real life. Now, in the middle of my second decade of marriage, we are still benefiting from my reading habits. Something new and interesting to try comes up now and again."

Reader Elemental admits that he "initially read romances as a teenage boy for the naughty bits. But even then, there was something useful. They planted the ideas that women can be just as sexual as men, that things like oral or foreplay aren't 'unmanly,' and a bit of sensitivity and willingness to communicate honestly can avoid a lot of aggravation later on. The actual sex-ed material I got elsewhere was all about the bare mechanics, so romances were largely my introduction to the emotions that accompanied the act, and confirmation that, yes, women actually enjoyed sex as much as men did."

"I learned a lot early on about what's good for a female, and that sex can and should be good for the female, and applied it in real life. Now, in the middle of my second decade of marriage, we are still benefiting from my reading habits. Something new and interesting to try comes up now and again."—NADIA, A READER

A reader who asked that I not reveal her name says that romance helped her get her adventure-sex merit badge (I only wish there were such a thing): "Reading romances really opened my eyes to the infinite possibilities of location. On more than one occasion my then-boyfriend-now-husband and

I availed ourselves of the woods in a public park, in every room in every apartment or house we've had (including laundry room and kitchen), in parked cars (and vans), in swimming pools and hot tubs, on conference room tables (oh, if his bosses had any idea…), and, most memorably, multiple times in the attic window of a campus building at the Naval Academy with my bare ass perched on the window sill."

Author Eve Savage found the sexuality of erotic romance had a lasting effect on her marriage, even before she began to write. Savage said that as her "life and reading tastes evolved, I started reading erotica which opened up a whole new world to me and my husband. Things we'd thought, but never had the guts to talk about or try, were now described in black and white. They helped us add new joys to our sex life and brought us closer together in the pleasure we give one another. Thirteen years of marriage and it's only getting better!"

"The actual sex-ed material I got elsewhere was all about the bare mechanics, so romances were largely my introduction to the emotions that accompanied the act, and confirmation that, yes, women actually enjoyed sex as much as men did."—ELEMENTAL, A READER

Even if the sexual possibilities seem impossible or downright uncomfortable in a novel, exploring your own sexuality in fiction can be very liberating—and, I won't lie, quite titillating. Jess Granger says that she "started reading romances at the age of thirteen or fourteen, right when I started getting curious about everything, but I wasn't quite sure what to do with myself, literally and figuratively.

"At the time, romances were fairly Old Skool, and some of them were over the top. One scene in Johanna Lindsey's *Savage Thunder* in particular stuck with me, and it wasn't until I was much, much older that I had the mental capacity to ask the question, 'Where would the saddle horn go?' Then I realized that probably wouldn't be very comfortable.

"I love the idea that sex in romance novels encourages us to explore new places. Okay, I'm not in a hurry to be that couple caught on the JumboTron at the ball game humping in the stands, but there's something to be said about a bit of controlled risk."

One of the more empowering and, in my never-humble opinion, awesomely excellent things about sex in romance is that the woman is not punished or ultimately harmed for being curious or even assertive about her sexual needs. Even in the Old Skool days of forced seductions and other questionable scenes, the wages of sex were not death, ostracism, misery, poverty, and complete moral turpitude. Getting some didn't mean giving yourself away—and it didn't mean you were done for once you did the deed. Sex has always been one of the major focuses of romance, even if an individual book contained only the chastest of kisses, because romances are about the heroine, and about her self-discovery and her happiness. That has to include sex—and the exploration and enjoyment thereof!

> "Sex in romance novels encourages us to explore new places."—ANONYMOUS, A READER

Jess Granger says reading the spicier romances, even those with sexually aggressive heroes, helped her as a young woman in immeasurable ways: "As a young girl discovering her sexual self, it kept me out of a lot of trouble. Since I could explore those issues and feelings through the books, I did not have the urge to try to figure them out with some pimply-faced awkward boy in homeroom. Let's face it. None of them were Fabio. Also, in a lot of those books, sex was scary! Oh, the pain! Not to mention the fact that so many of those poor heroines seemed to end up pregnant after one go.

"I didn't end up losing my virginity until I was nearly twenty-two and by that time romances were coming into the golden age of less rapeyness. Yay! At that point, I had discovered my sexual agency. The things I did, I did because I wanted to do them for me. They were my experience, not something I did to impress or cling to some schmuck.

"I had a sense of what I wanted from a man. I'll be honest—I wish I'd known that when I first encountered the opportunity, the means, and the possibility of having actual sex. I'd have saved myself a lot of misery—but then, I wasn't reading as much romance then."

Granger was also wise in the Romance as Sexual Research department. She says that reading romances "really contributed to sexy fun times...I had expectations there that were probably a tad unrealistic, but I knew that they were unrealistic so it wasn't an issue. It meant that I knew what I wanted and that I was comfortable asking what he wanted and saying what I wanted, and I don't think I would have been that relaxed in the situation if I hadn't read so many romance novels."

Research-devoted folks reading romance get a double-whammy of education. A reader named Pharaby explains that she "was fascinated by the sex, of course, and since I was a nerdy little bibliophile, I had research skills at my command to look up 'climax' and 'bordello' and 'erection'—using real books and paper card catalogs, no less.

"Also, 'tumescence.' Tumescence was very popular in the '80s. (I didn't learn the term 'whiskey dick' until I was in college, and that was, alas, not from a romance.)"

Another fringe benefit to reading sexually charged books with strong romances and strong heroines? They make you want to kick ass, take names, and have make-up sex afterward. Sharon S. says that "reading a really romantic and sexy book will put me in the mood for some lovin'. I just started reading paranormal romance and urban fantasy romance over a year ago and I could kick myself for not starting earlier."

Reader Milena agrees. While she reads mostly science fiction and fantasy and very Old Skool romances with the perspective that, as she puts it, "this is fun but nobody would want that in real life," she says that modern contemporary romances have proven quite useful: "Sex in modern romances is in fact much more interesting…and yes, more informative."

Reader James Lynch specifically mentioned attention to sexuality, or, as he put it, "kinkiness," in an online discussion of heroic traits. Sexuality, from Lynch's perspective, can be heroic: "There's one trait that hasn't been mentioned, and may not be a strict requirement, but is nevertheless fun: kinkiness. This lack may be due to so many heroines being naive innocents (while the men are sexually experienced—a literary standard going back to *Tom Jones*), but it's fun when the characters realize that there's more to sex than a bed with him on top.

"It's also fun when the heroine realizes that she's sexy. So many male characters ooze confidence and certainty while the

> Another fringe benefit to reading sexually charged books with strong romances and strong heroines? They make you want to kick ass, take names, and have make-up sex afterward.

female characters have no idea how beautiful/sexy they are but are instead rather shy and modest. There's a nice scene in *Love in the Afternoon* by Lisa Kleypas where the normally modest-dressing heroine gets a sexy bit of lingerie for her wedding night and shows herself off to her husband—leaving him stunned."

One problem with discussing romance and the sexual and physical elements in each novel—and the reader response to those elements—is that it possibly adds fuel to the nasty fire of accusation that romances are nothing but pornography for women. This is categorically not true. Romances are not porn. But they do contain sex. So did *NYPD Blue*, *Deuce Bigalow: Male Gigolo*, and the BBC's *Coupling*—and those are not pornography either. The presence of sex does not equal the definition of porn.

"I was frequently, even from the age of about eight, just as attracted to the women in the romance as the men. And it and a few other things helped me to acknowledge my sexuality and be OK with it. Romance helped me learn that the emotional journey in *any* relationship is just as important, if not more so, than the sexual destination."—CAITLIN, A READER

But then again, is frank discussion, depiction, or even description of sex automatically pornographic, or automatically a bad thing? I say no on both counts. Open and honest sex is a good thing, especially as depicted in erotic romance. Sonya agrees: "I know that some people hate the porn/romance novel comparison, but I've used both to introduce sex-related subjects with my boyfriend. 'Is this something you'd like?' 'We could totally do that position.' 'Those stockings would look really sexy on you.' 'I love it when you do that.' Romance and erotica aren't as good as porn for introducing positions or outfits, but they're much better than porn for role-play or toy suggestions and introducing kinkier subjects."

Professor Sarah Frantz says that, "yes, romances totally taught me about sex. They taught me about owning my own orgasm. They taught me about experimenting. They taught me about BDSM sex, about anal sex, about public sex, about making sure both partners enjoy it. They taught me about having *fun* during sex. About talking about sex and during sex. I may or may not have practiced some of what I learned, but it's all important knowledge."

Reader Caitlin saw her own sexuality in romance, and says it helped her understand her true self: "I was frequently, even from the age of about eight, just as attracted to the women in the romance as the men. And it and a few other things helped me to acknowledge my sexuality and be OK with it. Romance helped me learn that the emotional journey in *any* relationship is just as important, if not more so, than the sexual destination, and I think they helped with my self-respect in relationships later. Also, the well-written filthy ones *really* turn me on, which is good."

Seeing your own sexuality, and your own sexual self, in a novel can be tremendously liberating, and intimate. Merrian says that "the sexuality of modern romance novels has been a big help to me in reclaiming my own sexuality, which has been damaged by disability. Romance novels normalize desire and physical pleasure as a central part of love relationships. They have helped me strengthen my sense of entitlement to this. I feel more sexually confident because reading romance novels has helped me set boundaries, defining what is in, as well as what is out. They have also at times been a practical guide."

One benefit to the explicitness of romance is that, unlike movies or other visual media, the reader can *imagine* the people getting funky in funky positions—and can perhaps picture herself doing the funky without actually doing so. It's, as has been stated earlier, a safe space to explore without taking a risk or, say, entering a club devoted to BDSM with no knowledge of that practice or how it works. It's a lot less intimidating to read and experience in a book before one views and experiences in person that which is sexually challenging and alluring.

But then, even discussing sexual desires openly can be challenging, and certainly isn't a skill or talent that is cultivated easily. There are few easy manuals or patterns to follow for honest relationships or even for sexual encounters.

Reader and reviewer RedHeadedGirl says that the how-to

aspects of romance novels are not to be undervalued. She learned "first and foremost (I was in my early teens), the nuances of sex. I knew the mechanics, of course—tab A goes into slot B—and I suppose boobs work in there…somehow? But with romance, the varieties of the act, foreplay, and female orgasm (took me a while to figure that out—things like 'shuddering climax' and 'shattering bliss' aren't that helpful if you don't know what it refers to) became clear and the heavens opened, and, well, here we are.

"TMI alert: I will also admit that romance helped convince me to give sex a second shot. (Two virgins + no idea what we're doing + unlubed condom = Not Good Times.) But I'd read about all this bliss and pleasure and stuff, so…surely it had to be better, right? Right? And lo, it was."

Amber G. agrees: "One of the most important things romance taught me was that I had no idea how sex/intimacy worked, aside from very standard 'insert pole A into slot B' sex-ed stuff. The kind of things that go on in romance novels, I had no idea how they worked, but it sure seemed to make the protagonists happy. It prompted me to do a great deal of research and look up how-to guides so I wasn't a bad kisser or a stunned starfish my first time. It's amazing how well a little research goes over with a partner, and what it does for your self-esteem when you have an idea what you're doing.

"Not that my first time wasn't a mess. As RedHeadedGirl said, Bad Times is two virgins. Research only goes so far before you have to learn hands-on. But, prompted by what I

XO

learned from romance, not only did we recover from that mess, we're getting married in June after over five years together. Not too shabby."

Let's face it: there are embarrassing questions, and Embarrassing Questions. Erotic content helps people avoid asking either of those two—and can help you learn new things every day, as Ell says: "I've started reading erotica for the first time, and I *finally* know what a butt plug is for."

Lyra agrees: "I thought of something I did learn from romance novels, especially erotic romance. I learned what my kinks were! Before, I had no idea why some men would turn me on and other men, who seemed equally decent and suitable, did not. But after reading a lot of romance novels, some of which made me think, 'Meh, this doesn't do it for me' and some of which made me think, 'Yowza! This does!' I have pretty much sorted out the kind of man I need. (And it has nothing to do with looks!)"

The vicarious experience of reading about sex in the confines of romance and courtship has helped many a reader. Author Tamara Hogan probably says it best when she writes, "Romance novels have helped me in real-life relationships in a number of ways, but foremost in my mind is with sexual agency and negotiation. I've been reading romances since I was maybe eleven or twelve years old, and long before I got into a situation where a boy wanted to kiss me—or I wanted to kiss a boy, and maybe wanted to do more—I'd read countless stories modeling ways to say yes and ways to say no. Dress rehearsal, as it were."

> "I thought of something I did learn from romance novels, especially erotic romance. I learned what my kinks were!"—LYRA, A READER

Here's the bottom line (ha!): romance novels can teach how to have good, satisfying, adventurous, and entertaining sex. If you think you're the only one on the planet who isn't sure how some aspects of sexuality work, let me reassure you, you are so not alone. Romance occupies a strange sexual spectrum, in that some heroines are utterly baffled by sex, and some are so adventurous you're surprised the laws of gravity apply to them. There is no limit to what you can learn sexually from a romance, whether it's how to flirt, or how to…well, you get the idea.

SEX ADVICE FROM ROMANCE HEROINES

So what do you do if your sex life isn't blowing your skirt up, pun intended? What if sex has become like brushing your teeth, a routine that's part of a schedule, a habit, or a chore? Or what if the idea of sex is so terrifying and intimidating you can't even wrap your head around it, much less wrap around someone else's head?

Those are big issues. Let's face it: sex is a big issue. So who better than romance heroines to help?

The first piece of advice any romance heroine will give you: be explicit. No, I don't mean start talking dirty out of the blue and telling your man to put his Aer Lingus in your yoni while you're having brunch with his grandparents. I mean, specifically, say what you want.

If you don't know what you want? Well, time to read a few romance novels.

Even though sex is often strewn unabashedly with hot and heavy hyperbole in romances, underneath all that heaving and thrusting is a very simple pair of facts:

1. In a romance, the heroine's sexual satisfaction is required.
2. Heroines and heroes are equal participants in their own satisfaction, usually by satisfying one another.

How does good romance sex happen? Same way good real-world sex happens: communication and experimentation.

When I say "be explicit" about what you want, I don't mean to start talking like you just took BonerPorn 101 and want to use every possible word for the penis in one sentence.[1] Just because erotic romances like to do this does not mean you should! I mean that you should and that you can say out loud what it is you wish your partner to do to you physically. Sometimes—often times—this is a very spicy turn-on for both

---

1   *"Take your mighty wang sticky pants doodle, and holding your one-eyed yogurt-slinging trouser snake, batter up with your sword o' mighty lovin'."*

parties. You hear yourself saying what you'd like to happen to your body, and then, it happens.

Some romance heroines can teach us plenty about owning one's sexuality—over and over again. Molly Jennings, the heroine of Victoria Dahl's contemporary romance *Talk Me Down*, is an erotic romance author who returned to her home-town with a major case of writer's block, only to find that reconnecting with her high-school crush, Ben, was plenty of inspiration to crank her engine, cre-atively and literally. Molly is definitely someone who takes an active interest in all matters sexual, so when it came time to write about sex in romances, I asked Dahl to ask Molly if she had any advice for the readers of this book. Ha! As if she wouldn't.

Above all, Molly recommends that you start your own motor, so to speak:

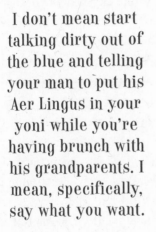

I don't mean start talking dirty out of the blue and telling your man to put his Aer Lingus in your yoni while you're having brunch with his grandparents. I mean, specifically, say what you want.

"My advice is simple: When it rains, it pours. If you're feeling lonely and sexually frustrated, there's a simple solution to the problem. Don't be. Take care of it yourself, ladies. There is nothing more appealing than a woman who's already plump with satisfaction. That's why men approach more often when you're happily involved in a relationship. You're confident and satisfied and sexy. Men can *see* that. They can feel it. It's oozing out of your pores. So make it ooze on your own. Wait...that didn't sound right. What I mean is that you should take your sexual satisfaction into your own hands. Buy a toy. Buy several toys. More importantly, use them.

"The next time you walk into a party by yourself, you'll look like you have a sexy secret. Best case scenario: men will be buzzing around you like bees. Worst case scenario: you're already relaxed and happy, so who cares what the men do anyway?"

—Molly Jennings, heroine of
Victoria Dahl's *Talk Me Down*

Keely McKay from Lorelei James's Rough Riders series is also, well, open to and about sex. Keely is adventurous and experienced in the exploration of multiple venues for sexual pleasure. In other words, more than one man? Not a problem at all. The Rough Riders series is among the most erotic, explicit, and emotionally deft collections of romance, and since Keely is present in several other stories until she gets her own romance in *All Jacked Up*, I figured she had plenty to say about sexual confidence and women with sexual experience. James was kind enough to query her, and heh, I was *so* not wrong:

"There's no such thing as a slut. That term pisses me off, like it's a fuckin' sin to love sex if you're a woman. How in the hell are you ever supposed to get good at something if you don't practice it? A lot? And who made up the asinine rule that you can only be with one guy, at one time? Puh-leaze. There's something very empowering about bending two men to your will—or bending over for them and seein' how fast those belt buckles fly. It's the ultimate rush being the sole focus of two mouths, two sets of hands, two cocks. Every woman should experience that a time or twenty in her life.

"But if you are a woman who insists on a one-on-one connection with your man, that doesn't mean it's gotta be boring, shut the lights off, missionary position, is-it-Saturday-already type of vanilla sex. Getting nekkid with him should be your priority. It'll drive him crazy when you take the lead and fuck him stupid. But don't expect your guy to be a mind reader. Tell him exactly what you want him to do to your body in as explicit and simple terms as possible.

"For God's sake, don't buy him a book on how to sexually please a woman, because what man willingly reads any kind of how-to manual? Even if there are raunchy step-by-step pictures. Be bossy. Be bold. Break out the porn and the sex toys to provide examples.

"That said, if you're used to being in charge in your life outside the bedroom, there is power in surrendering your body and your sexual will to your lover completely. Relying on him to provide you with what you crave in bed is not about love or companionship, but gorging yourself on as many banging-the-headboard orgasms as you can take.

"Who doesn't want a sex life that causes your secret smirk and his sexy swagger? I do. You should too. And darlin', the only way to get that well-fucked feeling, is to make it happen."

—Keely McKay, heroine of Lorelei
James's Rough Riders series

Bottom line (pun intended): Excellent sex, much like happiness, is something most everyone wishes to attain. And much like happiness, excellent sex takes some effort, though the payoff is absolutely worth it.

We Know How to Solve Problems

······· ♥ ·······

Romance novels are full of conflict. Why else would you want to read about the same few people for three hundred pages if there wasn't drama to be had, savored, experienced, and solved? An entire romance where Nothing Happens would be dull indeed.

The awesome thing about romance conflict is that it can be *so* completely ridiculous. Really. There can be some absolutely crazypants reasons for bringing the hero and heroine together. It's no accident that most romance novels don't often feature a "singles scene," either. Most of the time, the couple in a romance find themselves together whether they like it or not, mostly due to conflict, drama, and massive wtf-ery.

Consider the ways in which romance novel characters meet, and the problems that are created:

- In a bar when the heroine's ex-boyfriend bets that the smoothest guy he knows won't be able to get her phone number (Jennifer Crusie, *Bet Me*)
- At a formal ball in front of everyone they know, with not only their mothers but their grandmothers, great aunts, and assorted siblings in attendance (any number of historical romances)
- In an antiques shop where he tries to offend her with an obscenely decorated timepiece, and she not only buys the watch but the figure he was after as well (Loretta Chase, *Lord of Scoundrels*)
- At work, sort of, where she's the state's attorney working on a case and he's the police officer in charge, and they reconnect when she overhears a murder and he's assigned to the case (Julie James, *Something About You*)
- At her family home when he's sent to marry her, sight unseen, because of a contract his father made, and she's so appalled she dresses up so she's 200 percent more fug-ugly, just to repel him (Catherine Coulter, *Midsummer Magic*)
- Next to her trailer after he's directed to protect her (Patricia Briggs, *Moon Called*)
- In a cold, abandoned castle where he's been hiding, and she's been sent to kill him (Kresley Cole, *A Hunger Like No Other*)
- On a highway when she's dressed as a giant beaver (Susan Elizabeth Phillips, *Natural Born Charmer*)

- In a parlor when she shoots him with his own gun (Georgette Heyer, *Devil's Cub*)
- Under a tree when he falls drunkenly off a high branch onto her lap (Julia Quinn, *Brighter Than the Sun*)
- In a side parlor at a ball after she punched out some grabby-handed bonehead (Julia Quinn, *The Duke and I*)
- In a mountain cabin, unnerved but trying to be brave when a man shows up like an angry bear and wants to know what she's doing sleeping in his bed (Jill Shalvis, *Instant Attraction*)

See? Piece of cake! Just put together your romance-novel-inspired hunting kit. If it works for them, it'll work for you. Just acquire a gun, a beaver suit, a betrothal agreement, some super glue, some Shakespeare, a bawdy antique, and go punch out and then shoot the person of your dreams. If only it were that easy to find a good beaver suit.

After they meet, is it a short hop, skip, and a jump to happily-ever-after? Of course not. That would be boring and utterly unrealistic.

Then again, the problems that romance protagonists face can be really quite cumbersome:

- He's undead, immortal, and wants to kill her.
- The two of them must cohabitate or marry or both for upward of a calendar year to inherit big bucks-no whammies cashola in the amount of incredible wealth from a deceased and postmortem manipulative relative. (I have long said I want to get a law degree and specialize in *just* that kind of will and testament, the kind that *force* people to marry.)
- They have been betrothed to one another since birth, or since the nuchal fold test at twelve weeks gestation—and of course they hate each other.
- He won her in a poker game with her wastrel piece of shit father and has to marry her or she faces ruin and he faces destitution, which is almost the same thing, except not.
- Her ex-husband, who is completely and utterly crazy, is stalking her across the country.
- Two words: Serial. Killer.
- They are working the same legal case from opposite sides of the bench.
- He's a janitor; she's a nun.
- They agree to pretend to be a couple, possibly even a betrothed one, and then break off the engagement at a set time, but of course they fall for one another.
- He is buying her father's company, and he's only doing it because he hates her old man, but secretly he lusts in his pants for her.

- It was supposed to be a one-night stand.
- He's on a brief leave from active duty service.
- She has PTSD.
- She's a werewolf.
- He's the DJ; she's the rapper.
- They had a Big Misunderstanding.
- If they have sex, the world will be destroyed.
- If they don't have sex, the world will be destroyed, but they can't stand each other.

See? No shortage of conflict, problems, and obstacles to overcome, from the possible to the patently ridiculous. Yet beyond the ridiculous (and the heaving bosoms), romance novels create a space where every problem is solved and any conflict is worked through until it's not such a conflict any more, or, at the least, it's bearable and won't harm the happy ending for the characters. Stuff gets worked out, and tough conversations are had in romance novels, all with beneficial results. So even if he's an alien with the power to bench-press a building while undressing the heroine with his prehensile Jefferson Starship, the differences between them will be settled—and a hopeful, optimistic ending will be found.

There's a lot to learn from courtship and conflict resolution. When readers witness communication crises, and even big silly misunderstandings, they learn from the fictional example. Author Darlene Marshall says that romances are great for adjusting perspective to what matters and what can be a smaller (though often painful) problem: "I think reading romance novels, especially during rocky periods of my life when we had financial or health issues, helped me refocus on what's really important. Too often I think we can end up in stale relationships, especially those of us who've been married since dinosaurs roamed the planet. Sometimes reading a great romance reminds me life is about the people we love, and that together we can weather crises and come out better for it."

A reader who goes by the online handle Brussel Sprout says, "Romances established firmly in my mind that love is something worthwhile, worth hanging on for, and worth nurturing when you find it. Yes, the Emmentaler and Roquefort could be heavily layered, but the possibility that love can work is one that encouraged me to believe that I too would be able

> Most often, in a romance novel, the hero and heroine aren't looking for someone when they meet each other. In fact, amazing romance is often created when the two people aren't sure they like each other that much, but get stuck together—sometimes even literally. Perhaps you might want to pack a little super glue in that beaver suit...just a thought.

to have a sensible, sustainable relationship. I've been together with my husband for twenty years, married for sixteen, and I know that without romance novels, my love life would have been more chaotic and messy."

Plus, adds Shannon, seeing so many relationships intimately in fiction means additional clarity for her own relationships too: "When I was in a relationship that wasn't working out, I think that I was able to assess things to figure out what was wrong more easily because I had read so many romance novels and had seen so many different types of relationships. Not to say that I started viewing my relationship as a story or something like that, but I could realize that, hey, our only communication this week was that text four days ago. This is a problem."

Liz Talley agrees: "I do agree that romance books promote communication as the root of a healthy relationship. Very seldom do you see this to be false in a romance book."

Reader Amanda sees romances as a lesson in speaking up, and not avoiding the scary, difficult, awkward conversation, especially when the plots are a little ridiculous: "I think many romance novels are a lesson in What Not to Do, because so many involve the same plotline: Eyes Meet, Love, BIG MISUNDERSTANDING, HEA. And, like anyone else, what always gets me is how avoidable the Big Misunderstanding is. All anyone ever has to say is, 'Are you a spy?' 'I heard you killed your last wife,' or 'Did you make a bet that you could sleep with me within a month?' I think romance novels have taught me to just be brave and throw the words out there in the first place. At least then everyone is on the same page."

Reba says that the depictions of women and men in romances are actually, in her opinion, more liberated emotionally and sexually than in other forms of entertainment: "I didn't expect real men to be the same as romance novel heroes, any more than I expected them to be the same as fantasy novel heroes (and let's face it, no man is going to live up to Aragorn, no matter how awesome he is), but one thing I found surprising was how sympathetic I was to the men.

"They had feelings, thoughts, doubts, fears, stupid habits that got them into trouble. Their strength did not mean they were invulnerable. The most common tropes of movies, television, magazines, etc., about how men were or should be did not take into account their humanity until well after romance novels did. Male vulnerability was either a sign of weakness or illness, or the result of a devastating event—not part of the normal, everyday world of men as human beings. Yes, I'm generalizing, but the exceptions only prove the rule.

Looking to find your perfect match? Do it romance-novel style! Just acquire a gun, a beaver suit, a betrothal agreement, some super glue, some Shakespeare, a bawdy antique, and go punch out and then shoot the person of your dreams. If only it were that easy to find a good beaver suit.

> "I think romance novels have taught me to just be brave and throw the words out there in the first place. At least then everyone is on the same page."—AMANDA, A READER

"It seemed to me that men were liberated in romance novels long before they were in other media. So reading romance made me a little more sensitive to things my partner might not be showing or able to put in words. While it would be no fun if fictional characters opened up and solved things right away…romance novels taught me that open communication could work wonders."

Sometimes, it's the portrayal of the hero or heroine that causes the problem for the reader, one that can be overcome with a dose of common sense, reality, and humor. Some readers of romance do fall prey to the idea that Mr. Perfect will show up spontaneously, riding on a white horse (of course, of course), with marvelously groomed and suspiciously perfect hair and effortlessly minty breath, and as a result they miss some perfectly wonderful men in their real lives.

Kerrie says that her romance habits weren't helpful initially, but were a huge asset when it came to real relationships: "The romances I read throughout high school and even into college didn't do me any favors because they pushed that Mr. Perfect image that can never EVER exist in real life. I chased that ideal

> "I think reading romance novels, especially during rocky periods of my life when we had financial or health issues, helped me refocus on what's really important."
>
> —DARLENE MARSHALL

for a while and finally wised up when I found a totally imperfect but wonderful guy. One thing that those books did teach me, however, was communication! It can shorten the length of any misunderstanding."

Of course, authors have learned from the experience of writing through conflict and witnessing it solved in their own lives. Romances have helped Debbie Macomber with her own relationships. She says: "Reading romance novels and writing them, too, has given me an optimistic attitude, a recognition that if a couple cares enough, they can work through their conflicts. I can honestly say that romance novels have helped me think positively about my Wayne. We have our differences, but we're a team, working together toward our shared goals."

Teresa Medeiros says that her own parents' romance inspires her every day: "My own parents have spent fifty-plus years of marriage dealing with my mom's bipolar disorder. When my dad said, 'For better or worse, in sickness and in health,' he meant it. Even though she's now in a nursing home suffering from dementia, when he looks at her, he still sees the beautiful, brilliant girl he fell in love with all those years ago. That makes it so much easier for me to imagine my own characters growing old together while that first spark of passion deepens to a glowing ember, strong enough to last a lifetime."

> "Reading romance novels and writing them, too, has given me an optimistic attitude, a recognition that if a couple cares enough, they can work through their conflicts."
>
> —DEBBIE MACOMBER

Christina Dodd says she receives a lot of comments from readers about hope and validation, and the possibility that bad things will get better, and that real and hurtful problems can be solved: "Readers thank me for giving them hope. This always makes my heart trill. Women, especially in these tough times, are getting the shit end of the stick, especially when they're divorced or widowed or somehow left alone to raise their children. My stories are always about women who start out disadvantaged: poor, alone, helpless, badly treated, hopeless—any and all combinations. My heroines struggle against desperate odds, do what has to be done, and they make their way through the bad times until, by the end of the book, they have the life they want, the relationship they want, and the best sex in the history of the world. My heroines don't usually start out strong, but they grow, change, and become the kind of people we readers strive to be. Readers thank me for shining a light on their own struggle and making them see the light at the end of the tunnel.

"Am I offering false hope? Well, I've been in the tunnel; it was a bitch to get out, but I'm on the other side. So it is possible."

Dodd cautions that one single conversation would never really work to clear everything up as it does in a conveniently plotted novel: "I occasionally see readers online complain about romances in which any problems between the hero and heroine could be cleared up with 'one open, honest conversation.' And I think, 'You know nothing about relationships. You've never been in one in your life.'

> **"To talk about your problems with a beloved is an act of unimaginable courage. Words are powerful things; they can create or void trust, generate joy or pain, wound or heal."**
>
> —CHRISTINA DODD

"As far as I'm concerned, to say, 'The hero and heroine can clear up their problems with one conversation,' is simplistic. Any author worth her beans is presenting the progress of a realistic relationship. Every relationship starts with both parties pretending they're normal, witty, healthy, whole. As the relationship progresses and the hero and heroine get to know each other, the facade breaks down and truth starts leaking through. When a person has suffered physical and emotional trauma, to speak of that trauma is an act of unbelievable bravery, especially in a new, fragile, untried relationship. It's a talk that has to be conducted for the relationship to flourish and true love to grow, but will the person you love so deeply scoff at your trauma? Laugh? Turn away? The uncertainty, the pain, and the anguish make it easier to avoid that conversation, even to turn away from the relationship rather than say anything. To talk about your problems with a beloved is an act of unimaginable courage. Words are powerful things; they can create or void trust, generate joy or pain, wound or heal."

Kresley Cole says that reading about conflict and how any problem might possibly be solved can inspire readers to want more from their own relationships, and that seeing their own lives reflected in their fiction is a valuable experience for them: "They've thanked me for inspiring them to want—and to demand—more from their relationships. Which is a huge compliment since I take great pains to depict heroines who know what they want and refuse to settle for a 'hero' who hasn't earned the title (by being truthful with her, respecting her needs, and demonstrating a willingness to make sacrifices for the sake of their partnership)."

Repeatedly reading about courtship and the problems facing each one also allows readers to see and consider problems that are solved in myriad patterns. This is part of the reason why romance readers turn to the stories of courtship again and again.

Painful issues that are present in modern life are also present in romance novels. Eloisa James incorporated the feelings surrounding infertility and feeling a desperate desire to have a child into her own books, which are set a few hundred years in the past, long, long ago, in a setting far, far away from modern scientific advancements: "I tend to put real grievances into the stories of my marriages, along with real fears. But I also look at my friends' marriages. The best example is probably *Your Wicked Ways*. When I wrote that novel I had several close friends experiencing the pain of infertility, and going through the lengthy, painful medical processes that hope to reverse it. But their passion for motherhood was so strong that they were forging ahead, needles, hormones, and all.

"So that made me wonder what it would be like to feel that passionately back in the Regency period—if you were separated from your husband. What about if you were not only separated, but he was living with his mistress? And what if he said the only way he would impregnate you (to put it bluntly) was if you moved in the house along with the mistress? Would my friends have done it? Yup. So Helene did as well.

"That was a tough marriage to mend. Rees was terrible in bed and had to learn, slowly, how to actually make love as opposed to have sex. I have gotten a tremendous amount of mail about Rees over the years: many readers say it's their favorite book; others hate him and can't imagine why Helene fell back in love with him. A significant number have written to me about Rees's attitude toward sex and how it parallels men they've met over the years."

Seeing bad relationships improved can also help identify bad relationships in reality. Reader MD says that she "grew up with a very dysfunctional (and conservative) family, and for a while I liked the typical 'big misunderstanding' plots. From my point of view, they reflected reality. Plus the bodice rippers seemed to reflect some sort of reality as well, in the sense that the woman was the 'good girl' overcome by a hero or her own passion.

"The big change came for me when I started reading romance discussion boards, and heard people saying that such heroes are jerks in real life, and 'why they don't just talk to each other.' Seeing these reactions from other people opened for me a new way to look at things. Eventually, it motivated me to get into therapy and learn better patterns and better relationships."

One thing to remember, even in the fantasy-ripe environment of romance novels, is that not all problems can be solved. Sometimes, identifying them is enough of a lesson.

Author Sarah MacLean has a cautionary

perspective. In real life, it's not always possible to expect some-one to make a huge change—though it can be done. And that possibility of hope is its own motivation, whether it's motiva-tion to read another page, or try another day: "Ninety percent of the time, in real life, a relationship is not going to change bad behavior. I must confess that I hold firm to the belief that, in general, leopards (or leopardesses) do not change their spots: neurotic, untrusting women will always be neurotic and untrusting; possessive, dominating men will always be domi-nating; laziness and lack of motivation does not go away; and cheaters will always lean toward cheating.

> "Romance novels help with perspective: 'Yes, my husband's out of work, but at least my virginity was never wagered by a wastrel father in a card game!'"
>
> —COURTNEY MILAN

"Of course, romance novels are built on the idea that love conquers all and that a great relationship can evolve a hero or a heroine out of bad behavior and into the light—reformed rakes make the best husbands, do they not?

"And the truth is that we all have these people in our lives—the reformed rake who found love and monogamy, the slacker who found love and a career, the domineering alpha who is now a pussycat, the untrusting girl who, through love, has come to believe in herself and her appeal. These obstacles (however insurmountable) have been tackled; these stories (however rare) are real. And they give us hope. Which is perhaps why they make such excellent reads."

> "I also think that romance novels are valuable not just for the romantic relationship, but for the value that they place on community and friendship and belonging."
>
> —COURTNEY MILAN

Romances also serve as a lovely reality check, as author Courtney Milan explains: "Romance novels help with perspective: 'Yes, my husband's out of work, but at least my virginity was never wagered by a wastrel father in a card game!'

"I also think that romance novels are valuable not just for the romantic relationship, but for the value that they place on community and friendship and belonging. In our world, it's so easy to just disappear and be alone, and it's always important to have the reminder that no matter how bad things seem, it will always be better with good friends and family."

Kidnapping and dukes aside, when real and painful issues

are addressed in romances, it can be terribly reassuring and comforting, as reader Teshara can attest: "*This Is All I Ask* by Lynn Kurland is the first romance I read in my adult life and it really did change my outlook on relationships.

"It's OK to be traumatized. It's OK to have PTSD. It's OK to have flashbacks. It's OK to be broken. It's OK to be afraid of life. And it's OK to not be able to change these things on your own. It's OK to question your motivation for loving another person. It's OK to question why that person loves you.

"And the person you end up being with doesn't have to be 'normal.' Sometimes you can only trust people that have been through what you have, and you end up growing strong together instead of having to go it alone."

Romances provide hope and comfort that when things are really awful in the present, they will get better. Alpha Lyra writes that romances served a very crucial purpose in her life: "I didn't start reading romance until after my twelve-year marriage fell apart due to my husband's infidelity. Those years during the deterioration of the marriage and the divorce proceedings were horrible. Night after night, I cried myself to sleep.

"Romance novels not only gave me comfort during these awful times; I think they helped shield me from becoming cynical about love and thinking that all guys will eventually betray me. They made me willing to try again. So I'm still looking for my real HEA."

"It's OK to be traumatized. It's OK to have PTSD.
It's OK to have flashbacks. It's OK to be broken.
It's OK to be afraid of life. And it's OK to not
be able to change these things on your own.
It's OK to question your motivation for loving
another person. It's OK to question why that
person loves you."—TESHARA, A READER

You'd think all the happily-ever-after would be irritating to those facing or witnessing divorce, but Lyra isn't the only one who has used romances to face painful separations. Zisu writes, "In my teens, romance novels helped me deal with my disappointment in and sadness surrounding my parents' divorce and continued unpleasant relationship. They helped me believe in the possibility of an HEA, and escape from the disaster-EA I was part of."

Jessi credits romances with giving her a happy fantasy that contrasted enough with the painful reality of her parents' divorce that she was able to recognize potentially destructive habits: "My parents were divorced when I was five, and from that time on, every influential person in my life was divorced and excessively bitter. I also had some pretty extensive daddy issues due to my own father's frequent absences. However, I started reading romance when I was probably eleven or twelve (in secret, of course) and I truly believe that my obsession with the genre helped build my own belief in love and in the fact that not all men are dicks who should die a painful and prolonged death.

....

> "Romance novels not only gave me comfort during these awful times [after my divorce]; I think they helped shield me from becoming cynical about love and thinking that all guys will eventually betray me."—ALPHA LYRA, A READER

....

"Romance novels allowed me to imagine being loved by a man and thus to begin to see value in myself and demand that others see it as well. I grew up in a small town and almost all of my friends got married very early and now have lots of kids and a good number are divorced. I have managed to escape that life, find a profession that I love and which I am amazing at (I'm a librarian), and find the love of my life (we've been together eight years now). I attribute my success, my faith in myself, and my faith in love to my rabid reading habits in general and to the romance genre in particular. A little imagination goes a long way in overcoming most of life's problems."

Eloisa James has also written about how painful it can be to truly get to know someone intimately: "In my *Affair Before Christmas*, the young married couple are estranged because they simply don't understand each other in bed at all. And neither one has been totally honest with each other. I had to untangle a lot of family history in order to get them to a place where they could not only be in love, but make love. I think the key there was that the hero simply decided he loved his wife so much that he would be faithful to her, even if he never had sex again. That kind of faithfulness gave her the ability to trust him—and then to fall truly in love with him.

> "Romance novels allowed me to imagine being loved by a man and thus to begin to see value in myself and demand that others see it as well."—JESSI, A READER

"One thing that people don't do all that often is talk about male virgins. In *When the Duke Returns*, both the hero and heroine are virgins. Their first time, and second, aren't great. Because sex isn't all that great in the beginning. I got loads of funny mail about this, some of which was from women who'd slept with virgins (one had slept with four virgins, as I recall)."

While it's not always possible to cure jealous or suspicious men of their insecurities, it is possible to see that people can change and escape, for a time, people who do more harm than good, even without meaning to. James received a fan letter from a writer who said that one of her favorite parts of writing romance is that she is able to "repair those toxic people and relationships—even if it's only on paper."

Anna Campbell agrees: "Actually one of the things I love about a great romance is that it offers hope for overcoming seemingly impossible obstacles." Seeing those obstacles in other people's lives can also help create apprecia-tion of the strengths of one's own relationships when they are tested: "I suspect romance has contributed to my belief that if respect is lack-ing between me and my other, the relationship has no hope. Does that come from romance novels or from parents who brought me up to value myself? Who knows? It's certainly a good principle!"

Interestingly, Campbell's books include characters who start off on the opposite side of that spectrum—they usually believe themselves undeserving of happiness at all: "I think all my books include either a hero or a heroine, and sometimes both, who believe themselves unable to sustain a healthy relation-ship. Lone wolves lured back to the warmth of the campfire proliferate in Campbellandia. For example, in *Captive of Sin*, Sir Gideon Trevithick is convinced he's condemned to a life of pain, madness, and solitude. A normal life is forever out of reach. But when he enters a marriage of convenience with Charis Weston to save her from her greedy, vicious stepbrothers, she drags him kicking and screaming back into the human race."

Campbell has much better fan mail than Eloisa James, I'm amazed to say: "I've had several emails from readers kidnapped by Scottish dukes who have thanked me for my advice."

(She's kidding. I think.)

Nora Roberts also sees her own life through the lens of romance at times: "Writing romance novels has certainly helped me learn, discover, understand all sorts of angles and quirks in love, relationships, and men. While fictionalized, and by nature romanticized, a romance novel is a story about people and their emotional journeys. They can provide a great deal of insight into human nature, and the human heart.

"Honestly, every book I write, and certainly most I read and enjoy, teaches me a little bit more about relationships. How different people with different traits, backgrounds, needs, flaws, and so on come together, deal with problems, celebrate joys, handle all the ups and downs."

"Honestly, every book I write, and certainly most I read and enjoy, teaches me a little bit more about relationships. How different people with different traits, backgrounds, needs, flaws, and so on come together, deal with problems, celebrate joys, handle all the ups and downs."

—NORA ROBERTS

Author Nalini Singh says that great romance is based on the idea that happiness is not impossible: "I think the crux of a great romance is the belief that nothing is impossible. I've read about traumatized heroes and heroines, and I've read about paranormal worlds torn apart by war where the characters find love—for me, it is not so much the 'impossible obstacle' that is important, but whether the writer is able to make me believe in the outcome."

Reading romances and taking them literally is definitely *not* the path to everlasting happiness. There are some crazy over-the-top plots that would never fly in the real world. Just listen to Courtney Milan on this: "For any men who may be reading this, I don't generally advise looking to romance novels as an ideal way to woo a woman—if you like a girl, I suggest asking her out on a date, in preference to threatening to turn her ecologically sound tourism location into a strip mall."

But believing that the happy-ever-after and the happy-right-now are possible can create a powerful motivation to creating that happiness for oneself. The belief that things will get better is self-fulfilling. In a romance novel, things will always be OK in the end, and if they're not okay, it's not the end. The same can be said of real life: there is a second chance, another day, another opportunity to try again and make everything a little bit better, because happy endings take work.

We Know How to Ask
for What We Want

♥

Without a doubt, some of the most emotionally touching and satisfying scenes in a romance novel are when one character declares how he or she feels, either through words or actions. Here are some of the favorite scenes of well-read romance fans:

JUST ONE OF THE GUYS
BY KRISTAN HIGGINS
(HQN/Harlequin Ltd., 2008)
Suggested by Diane N.

"Chastity," he says quietly. "I can't live without you for another minute."

The mike falls to the dance floor with a thunk as I cover my mouth with both hands. Tears spill out of my eyes, and I can't seem to draw a breath. The room is absolutely silent.

"I've loved you my whole life, Chas, from that first day you took me home after Michelle died. And I'm terrified you'll leave me or you'll stop loving me or even worse, something will happen to you. But I can't be without you anymore."

HEAVEN AND EARTH
BY NORA ROBERTS
(Penguin/Berkley Jove, 2001)
Suggested by Megaera

"I don't want you here." She shoved at him, and her voice began to hitch. "I don't want you near me."

"Why?"

"Because, you moron, I'm in love with you."

He ran his hands down her arms, taking hers as he leaned over to touch his lips to her forehead.

"Well, you idiot, I'm in love with you, too. Let's sit down and start there."

THE DUKE AND I
BY JULIA QUINN
(Avon/HarperCollins, 2000)
Suggested by me

Her giggles exploded into full-throated laughter.

"Didn't anyone tell you not to laugh at a man when he's trying to seduce you?"

If she'd had any chance of stopping her laughter before, it was gone now. "Oh, Simon," she gasped, "I do love you."

He went utterly still. "What?"

Daphne just smiled and touched his cheek. She understood him so much better now. After facing such rejection as a child, he probably didn't realize he was worthy of love. And he probably wasn't certain how to give it in return. But she could wait. She could wait forever for this man.

"You don't have to say anything," she whispered. "Just know that I love you."

The look in Simon's eyes was somehow both over-joyed and stricken.

CARESSED BY ICE
BY NALINI SINGH
(Berkley/Penguin, 2007)
Suggested by Andrea

She turned to grab a couple of ice packs from the built-in cooler. "Sit."

"I said—"

"Sit."

He sprawled into a chair. When she wrapped the ice packs in a small towel and placed them against his ribs, he didn't protest. "What is it with men and testosterone?" she muttered, standing in the vee formed by his outstretched legs.

"I don't think you'd like us without it." He held the ice packs to his side by pinning them with his arm. "There was no need for this."

She was about to snap a comeback when she realized he'd come to her precisely because she'd fuss over him, no matter what he must've told himself to the contrary.

LAST NIGHT'S SCANDAL
BY LORETTA CHASE
(Avon/HarperCollins, 2010)
Suggested by me

> "Come," she repeated, patting the bedclothes. "I want to show you my treasures…"
>
> She opened the box and started taking them out: the packets of letters he'd written to her, the little painted wooden man—the first gift he'd sent her, the bracelet with the blue stones, the piece of alabaster… on and on. Ten years of little treasures he'd sent her. And the handkerchief with his initials she'd stolen a few weeks ago.
>
> She looked up at him, her eyes itching and her throat aching. "I do love you," she said. "You see?"
>
> He nodded, slowly. "I see," he said. "Yes, I see."

····· ♥ ·····

Asking for what you want can be very, very difficult.

In 2008, I started a regular advice column on the *Smart Bitches* website wherein relationship problems would be answered with the wit and wisdom of romance novels. In February 2010, I published the following letter, and am happy to say I have an update from the original correspondent.

Dear Smart Bitch Sarah:

I am a longtime lurker and I am in need of some advice. I have recently met a guy through an online dating site. We IMed every day for three weeks (we also talked on the phone) and then met in person. That meeting lasted the entire day. We continue to talk almost every day and have gone out again. I keep getting mixed signals from him. When we talk he sometimes references wanting a chance with me. But he is continuing to meet people on the dating site. Before we ever went out he told me he was a "friends first and see where that goes" kind of guy.

I am OK with that as that is how I operate. I just think that I would rather he didn't reference dating me and telling me he is going on a date with someone else in the same conversation. I would be OK just being friends with him, but I have the feeling that if I let this continue I am going to get hurt. Am I just deluding myself? Should I tell him that I can't continue this way? Should I just go with the flow and stop worrying? My feeling is if he really wanted a chance with me, then he's got it, and why is he dating other people? If he doesn't want a chance with me, then why does he keep mentioning it?

Sign me—So very confused

Dear So Very Confused:

In a romance novel, it's no secret or mystery that the hero will like the heroine and the heroine will like the hero, and at some point between them, lips and assorted other bits will meet. In real life, there's that pesky lack of omniscience to deal with. It's so annoying, especially when, as it seems from your letter, you're not sure what he wants…and you're not sure what you want, either.

I think there are two problems here. First: his definition of the word "dating" and your definition of the word "dating" may be two very different things. Does "dating" imply exclusivity or not? You seem to think you'd like it to, while his definition seems to be entirely different.

Second, what do you want? It sounds to me like you have a rather fun friendship with this guy, despite his mixed signals of "wanting a chance." You talk often; you see each other. You've told me a lot about what he's saying and what he's doing, but what about you?

So answer these questions: What do you want? What does "having a chance" mean? Is his referring to dating other women a question of manners and courtesy, or is it a question of your being unable to voice aloud that you'd like him to stop dating others and focus on you? Or do you want him to come to that conclusion on his own?

If he'd like to have a chance with you and he says so repeatedly, you need to spell out what has to happen for him to have the opportunity to be your boyfriend. If you'd rather be dating-as-maybe-friends, that clearly means, in his world, he will date other women and meet other women. If that bothers you, you need to speak up.

If you don't really want an exclusive relationship, then ask him to keep the details to himself. You can set the terms of conversation. If he sees you as a friend, then he feels comfortable telling you about other women he's seeing. But if he sees you as someone with whom he'd like a more meaningful relationship, telling you about other dates seems a strange thing to do.

If you want to stop worrying and wondering altogether, you need to figure some things out for yourself. First, ask yourself if you want an exclusive relationship with him. If you don't, then let him do his thing and you do yours, and ask him not to dish about other chicks he's dating as it bothers you a bit. If you do want that relationship, then speak up and tell him what you want.

He may keep mentioning the idea of being with you to gauge your reaction. He may be mentioning it because "having a chance" with you means getting you in bed. Who the hell knows? The only things under your control are your actions and reactions.

So: make your signals clear, and see how he responds. Decide if he is the one you want to take your chance on, and then offer him that chance he's been talking about—and explain the terms you're comfortable with. If he is what you want, go for it. A little miscommunication never hurt anyone, except when it adds two hundred pages of conflict when a simple conversation would have solved it.

Being the heroine of your own happy ending does require that you ask for what you want instead of waiting for it to come to you. Sometimes, figuring out what you want before you act on it is the harder of the two.

Lo and behold, a few months later, I emailed So Very Confused to ask whether she was still friends with this person, and things had changed. Her response: "I am actually dating the guy now. Amazing how a little of just asking the other person what's up will answer questions! Getting the guts to do so is another story…"

I asked her for her advice to anyone else in a similar situation, and she wrote:

I guess for me it was a matter of [needing] a yes or a no answer. I couldn't stand the not knowing any longer. I wrote to you in February but I didn't point-blank tell him how I felt until the end of May (I tried the "Let's go with the flow" method first). And I told him *exactly* how I felt and what I wanted. And he turned me down. Told me no.

And you know what? I survived. Yes, I was upset that first day but I had my answer. The twist to the story is that we continued to be friends (the friendship was that awesome—I still wanted to talk to him). Then about a month later he [came] to me and [said he'd] changed his mind. The last month of friendship [had] made him want to at least try a relationship. And we have been together ever since. The rule of open, honest, let-it-all-hang-out communication stands. And it works for us.

That is my story. I hit my breaking point and just went for it, nerves and all. It didn't go down how I wanted it to...but in the end it worked out. I will also say that after I was turned down I didn't just sit at home and wallow. I went out and did stuff (a road trip, kayaking, hiking, etc.) and I think that hearing about my many adventures also cleared his vision to just how cool I was. (Modest too ;-))

I'm not sure I can contain my own giddypants at Confused's happy ending. In order to be the hero of your own life, you have to decide what you want first. You are a person worth being with, and you should first and foremost be happy with yourself and have the confidence to say what it is you want.

And, as Confused points out, as scary as it is, you have to ask for what you want, or you'll never get it—you cannot expect anyone, male or female, friend or significant other, to read your mind and anticipate exactly what you want. You must speak up for yourself.

There's a terrible vulnerability in admitting how you feel and asking someone to admit their feelings in return. Most people are instinctively resistant to being vulnerable—including emotionally—but the payoff is almost always worth the risk. Even if that payoff comes later, as Confused demonstrates, when the person you've revealed yourself to has realized what a treasure you are.

If you're more than passingly familiar with romance

novels, though, you're probably raising a brow since part of the romance fantasy is often that the guy can anticipate the heroine's every desire—and in some novels knows what's best for the heroine before she does. In other books, the heroine decides she knows best and figures out how to bring the hero around to her thinking.

Ultimately, in just about each and every case, the characters figure out what they want and decide to go after it. This step in an active direction usually means revealing everything the person feels, and what that person wants. It's risky, but the payoff is worth the terror. Just ask Confused, who is, right now, happy she took the risk.

We Know That
Happily-Ever-After Takes Work

························· ♥ ·················

H ere is the number one lesson from romance novels. Ready? You've read this far, you might as well get the payoff now!

As I wrote earlier, happily-ever-after isn't sometime in the future. It exists right now, and starts with you. More importantly, courtship, the process of charming someone and demonstrating in word, thought, and action how much you care about them, does *not* end with the declaration of love or the commitment between you.

Courtship becomes part of relationship maintenance, but "maintenance" itself is a horribly unsexy word. Getting your oil changed as part of routine maintenance? Not fun. But getting the oil changed and the car washed on your significant other's vehicle? Now that's a very kind and lovely thing to do. That kind of care and thoughtfulness is what sustains the happy until, you'll pardon the bad and sickly sweet joke, it's never ending.

"Routine care and maintenance" are among the most unsexy and uninspiring words. Oil changes, annual physicals, and food and water do not always inspire passion or the remote possibility of poetry. While the absence of bad sonnets might be a good thing, the absence of care will wither a relationship faster than an orchid outside in an ice storm.

It's better to think of the care and feeding of your relationships as "courtship," only without that pesky insecurity of not knowing if the person feels the same way about you.

A very wise reader of Eloisa James's wrote to her, "I've come to believe that people need to fall in love more than once if they are to stay together." That is so very true. And while many romances are the depiction of falling in love once and for all, treating your personal romance as a repeated courtship keeps that relationship happy and healthy.

> While many romances are the depiction of falling in love once and for all, treating your personal romance as a repeated courtship keeps that relationship happy and healthy.

Is the never-ending courtship present in romance novels? Well, it's not exactly present in a single novel—but it is present in the entire genre, one happy courtship after another. Most romance novels end with the commitment. But if the details of a happily-ever-after aren't always written out explicitly in the text, how does the reader know, and more importantly believe, that the happily-ever-after is going to be happy in the

ever-after? Because both the hero and heroine have demonstrated that they know how to take care of the other person,
and of their relationship.

It is really bothersome when you read a romance and you
don't believe the hero or heroine understands how to make
a happy relationship work. With a romance where you don't
have confidence in the hero and heroine and suspect that when
things get tough, the hero or heroine couldn't find their own
ass with both hands, much less help one another, it is easy to
fear somehow that the happiness isn't going to last.

There are some people who couldn't spot and copy decent
behavior if they were programmed to do nothing but feed other
people's parking meters. The hero who remains assiduously
dedicated to his preference to jump to erroneous conclusions and
never seems to realize his own mistakes is not going to reassure
a reader of his eternal heroism. The heroine who is a selfish or
clueless cloud-living goofball who needs a man to save her every
third second because she will without fail investigate that strange
noise in the kitchen when the serial killer is on the loose and the
kitchen door is open—yeah, not so much with the confidence in
that person's ability to be an adult and care for an adult relationship. Idiocy and self-absorption are not heroic or inspiring.

Reading about couples who can successfully
weather just about any horrible thing, from death,
murder investigations, and blackmail to the possibility
of interplanetary collision brought about by not
enough kissing, gives readers confidence and
the belief that those two characters can survive

anything, and gives room for the possibility that any real problem can be solved too—with enough interplanetary gun battles,
of course. Author Toni Blake says that reading romances helps
her with her own real-life relationships because, "Reading
books that all come with a 'happily-ever-after' generally keeps
me working toward solutions in my own marriage, and seeing
things in a more positive light. Cumulatively, they send the
message that nothing is unsolvable.

"In my observation, sadly, in real life, most people don't
overcome truly huge relationship obstacles. But the point
of a romance novel is to make you believe that you can, to
help you see the possibility. Romance novels show people
ultimately sacrificing their pride, putting their hearts at risk,
exercising forgiveness, and exhibiting faith in the person they
love—not stupidly or blindly, but with the belief that love is
of great value and worth fighting for."

There's always another obstacle. Either that problem faces
both parties, or an internal struggle exists on one side, but
there's always another crapful difficulty to deal with. That's
why happiness as a present and abiding element to a relationship is so important: without it, those obstacles are impossible.
If people treated their relationships like an extended courtship,
and made it a point to demonstrate that they care about the
people they're with, overwhelming problems may not seem so
daunting because there's someone there to help.

One way to demonstrate courtship as a matter of course
in an established relationship is to remember that courtship
is the act of trying to persuade someone to choose you—by

demonstrating that you've chosen them. If you look at each day of your relationship as another opportunity to choose to be with the person you're with, you'll display those feelings of affection in your actions and your words—and you'll refrain from taking that person's presence for granted.

Author Courtney Milan says that another way to keep a relationship healthy is to feed it—but not in the way you might think: "In every romance novel I've written to date, there is a point when the hero feeds the heroine. Nothing elaborate (at least not so far)—but so far, my guys have made their women tea (in a novella) or bought oranges and bread (in a book) or brought her tea the morning after (tea is good; have you noticed?), or he's made her a hot toddy (in another book).

"Sometimes the trick to surviving the mountains of external crap that the world throws at you is to make sure that you share the little stuff."

> "In every romance novel I've written to date, there is a point when the hero feeds the heroine...Sometimes the trick to surviving the mountains of external crap that the world throws at you is to make sure that you share the little stuff."
>
> —COURTNEY MILAN

Debbie Macomber says that communicating affection in romance is not that different from communicating affection in the real world: "In my mind, a hero is basically a decent, honorable man. She makes him a better man, and he plays the same role in her life—making her a better woman. In each case, the relationship brings balance to their lives. They come to rely on and encourage each other to be the best people they can be.

"In every romance novel, there's a key transformation in both the hero and heroine as they learn the give-and-take of love, the importance of bending their wills to align with the will of the one they love. They need to believe in each other, to treasure their differences and appreciate what they have in common."

Author Sarah MacLean sees romance as a requirement for real relationships, and points to romance novels as an excellent reminder of what romance is: "I...find that romances have always helped me navigate bad relationships. While there's definitely a reason why romances end at the beginning of a relationship (dirty breeches on the bedchamber floor do not a sigh-inducing ending make), the idea that love and romance can and should be a part of a real-life relationship is not a bad one. And if we hold our relationships

> "You should never stop courting your spouse!"
>
> —TERESA MEDEIROS

up to that standard—the one where love and romance come along with the dirty socks and Sunday afternoon football sessions—it can only be better for all of us."

THE MEDEIROS CHARACTER TRAIT LIST

Teresa Medeiros has a list of traits she feels characters must possess before they can earn their happy endings, a list that easily applies to actual people too:

1. To earn their happily-ever-after, they have to learn to embrace their newfound love, flaws and all.
2. They must come to understand that people are the sum of all their past experiences, both positive and negative.
3. They must mature enough to surrender the "me" to become the "we."
4. And they must endure enough of the "worse" during the course of the book to appreciate the "better" to come. Medeiros says that romance novels have always reminded her "to keep the magic alive; you should never stop courting your spouse!"

Christina Dodd says that characters "have to take responsibility for their actions, both romantic and in the course of the plot, and be brave enough not only to fix what they've broken but admit they were wrong. Since most of us would rather walk on hot coals than admit we're wrong (at least I would), this is an agony that proves them worthy of love and their happiness." Those same developed skills can be found in real people as well, according to Dodd: "I see it all the time in real life and in every romance—men and women overcome their basic, intrinsic inability to communicate and form a lasting relationship. When you think about the differences between the genders, it's a freaking miracle."

> "The idea that love and romance can and should be a part of a real-life relationship is not a bad one. And if we hold our relationships up to that standard–the one where love and romance come along with the dirty socks and Sunday afternoon football sessions– it can only be better for all of us."
>
> —SARAH MACLEAN

Dodd also recommends communication, though for her, communication in her marriage means her husband reads her books: "I've been married to my husband since the earth's crust cooled. He was the one who supported and encouraged me through ten years of being unpublished, and he's read a lot of my books, about thirty. Since, in my opinion, most men don't have any ability (or see the need) to examine the way anyone else thinks (an aside—I don't believe most men know how *they* think), for my husband, reading the female point of view is a sort of, 'Here's a roadmap to the way a woman's mind, or at least Christina's mind, works.' It's led to interesting discussions."

Even with a roadmap, whether it's staggeringly honest conversations or a collection of over thirty different romance novels written by your spouse (lucky Mr. Dodd), without the conflict, there's no romance. Kresley Cole agrees: "Someone once asked me, 'When you're writing a romance, do you ever wish you could just have the hero and heroine meet, fall in love, and live happily ever after without all the heartache and hardships?'

"I answered that without all the heartache and hardships there would be no HEA, because at the outset of a book, my protagonists don't 'fit' well enough to sustain a lasting relationship. There can be attraction between them, maybe even a grudging respect for each other—but without all the trials they endure over the course of the story, the characters would remain unfinished. Those trials do two things: force the characters to grow, so they will be better able to maintain a partnership, and teach them the value of the relationship, so they never take it for granted.

"One thing I think most outside the genre don't realize is that romance protagonists earn their HEA. They have to work for it. I believe that above all things, romance novels teach us that HEAs don't come easy. As in real life, these relationships take effort, dedication, and sacrifice.

"An entirely distorted view of adult relationships would be the scenario from above: meet, fall in love, live happily ever after without any heartache. If romance novels perpetuated that distorted view, they'd all be ten pages long."

> "One thing I think most outside the genre don't realize is that romance protagonists earn their HEA. They have to work for it. I believe that above all things, romance novels teach us that HEAs don't come easy. As in real life, these relationships take effort, dedication, and sacrifice."
>
> —KRESLEY COLE

Author Anne Calhoun says that she sees the happily-ever-after as accepting imperfections, both in one's self and in someone else: "A common misperception about romance characters is that they have to be perfect, that they've earned their HEA because they are already sane, stable, thin, beautiful, ripped, honest, loyal, rich, and/or willing to risk it all for the person they love, but just need a little nudge to get their HEA. While authors have begun to write physically 'different' characters—perhaps 'curvy' (as if curves are somehow indicative of a character flaw…like enjoying food), or 'mousy' or 'librarian'—the characters that resonate most with me are the ones who are truly, deeply flawed and somehow manage to be loved for exactly who they are.

"Maybe that's the key thing for me. For me, characters 'earn' an HEA less than they 'accept' the HEA. I don't think we (or characters) earn love or happily-ever-afters. They/ we don't start out unworthy and become worthy. They/we start out muddled and become less muddled. If we writers do our jobs well, they start out human and become *more* human. Sometimes that acceptance comes from the hero or heroine loving them just as they are, and sometimes it comes from the hero or heroine learning something about themselves they need to know in order to move past their pain and become more fully alive and in love. That's what really makes romances great. The characters, after their trials and tribulations, are more fully alive, more fully engaged in the world, more fully human. They may live the exact same life, but inside they are changed.

"As a reader I want to see a character grow. I don't really care where they start from, or even where they end up, as long as that character has grown through the conflict faced and their interaction with the hero or heroine."

Sometimes, circumstances are tough and people are miserable, and big girl pants must be put on with aplomb so that the trouble can be dealt with, sword fighting optional. The effort and work to look at one's own faults is onerous, but any amount of self-examination can make a definite difference when things are in the crapper. Debbie Macomber has examined relationship repair tools in many of her books, most notably *Hannah's List*: "In my book, there's a couple, Winter and Pierre, who have gotten into a routine of fighting, separating, and then breaking up again. It's a pattern that's continued for years. They're in love, but they can't seem to get along. Another character suggests that Winter make a list of everything Pierre does that irritates her and then write down her reaction to that behavior.

> **"A common misperception about romance characters is that they have to be perfect, that they've earned their HEA because they are already sane, stable, thin, beautiful, ripped, honest, loyal, rich, and/or willing to risk it all for the person they love, but just need a little nudge to get their HEA."**
>
> —ANNE CALHOUN

"When she sees how she's nagged and pouted and exploded at him, she recognizes her own part in their troubled relationship. She persuades Pierre to do the same thing, and once they see what's happening to them they're able to resolve their problems and eventually marry. A reader wrote to tell me she'd used the same technique in dealing with a situation in her marriage, and it helped her and her husband tremendously.

"In addition, another character in *Hannah's List*, Michael, has to learn how to have a relationship with Macy, despite the fact that a) he's reluctant to have a relationship with anyone, and b) Macy is just so different from him—too different in his view. He's still grieving for his wife, Hannah, who left him a letter encouraging him to remarry, even providing him with a list of candidates, which included Macy. So, what drives the story emotionally is Michael's need to figure out how to see Macy on her own terms, not his, which means he has to see himself differently too. This was an interesting exploration for me, the author, as well as for Michael!"

Reader Sybylla agrees that recognition of past behavior and the possible need to change it can make a story extraordinary: "Something I do look for is that the hero/heroine challenges the other person in some fundamental way. It can be because he or she makes the other want to be a better person, or forces them to reevaluate their assumptions, or even just causes them to change their social behavior.

"One of the things that makes Mr. Darcy so appealing to me is his simple recognition that he had been rude, and that rudeness is not okay. To stick with Austen, I like *Persuasion* in part because both characters have to reevaluate their past behavior and question why they made the choices they did.

"In *Bet Me*, Cal challenges Min to accept herself and to see herself as desirable, while she forces him to take a closer look at how he's always acted with women."

Readers and authors also know that happiness doesn't just show up any more than great sex does. Happiness takes work. As Julia London says, "There are ebbs and flows to every relationship, and the trick is to weather the storms and head for calm seas. That sounds trite, but it is so true. Every relationship has its moments. Every couple has its faults. The couple has to work really hard to reach that happily-ever-after, in real life and in books."

Author Robyn Carr says the question of making a happily-ever-after work lies in the focus: "In a conversation with my grown son about the power of intention and a positive outlook on life, I posed the argument, 'But bad things do happen to good people.' And he said, 'Bad things happen to all people, but so do good things.' Focus becomes a compelling force in life, and in writing romances. Concentrating on the positive, on the good in life, and finding a way to get there makes for good relationships and a successful life."

Romance reader Jess Granger says, "My first real boyfriend didn't love me with a passion that could lead to my HEA. My second was all passion, but no substance. I knew he couldn't be the one to stand up for me and support or protect me. I found my husband later, a perfect balance of passion, friendship, and support.

"I recognized those things in him because romances made me think about what I wanted and what I liked in a hero...I learned how I wanted to be treated. I am reaping the benefits of having an open mind, enough sexual power and agency to communicate what I want, like, and need in the bedroom, and a knowledge that every couple has dark moments, but it's how you work through them that leads to your happy-ever-after."

Shannon H. agrees with Jess, and says that romances have helped her figure out that, for her, relationships were preferable to hooking up because she had learned how to create a happy one: "I started reading them when I was around eleven or twelve years old (I'm nineteen now), and immediately set super high standards for myself in what I wanted in a guy. Things like Treats Me Well, Spends Time with Me, Makes Me Smile, Compromises, etc. Things that are perfectly realistic, I feel. It made me choose to not settle when I could have done so just to say that I had a boyfriend, and being in college now I think romance has made me perfectly comfortable in turning down hook-ups in favor of an actual relationship."

Professor Sarah Frantz, romance reader and reviewer, says that romances have taught her similar lessons as Shannon has described: "Romances taught me everything I needed to know about how to communicate in a relationship and I credit them with my twenty-years-and-going-strong relationship with my partner. They taught me to make sure everyone got a say. They taught me to make sure everything was covered—everything. No hiding that one last little niggle. It all has to come out.

"They taught me how to discuss things. They taught me that the relationship, the 'us,' is paramount over the 'you and me.' They taught me to respect my partner at all times. And most of all, they taught me to appreciate my partner and to express that appreciation whenever possible. He brought me a cup of tea, whether or not I asked him for it? Thank him. And tell him I love him. It's the little, everyday gestures that show love more than the grand gestures, and romances taught me that."

Even classic romances such as those by Georgette Heyer can serve as a prototype for ideal behavior: a commenter at the site who goes by the name DreadPirateRachel told me, "The first romances I ever read were by Georgette Heyer. They taught me to hold out for a partner who would share my intellectual passions and respect me for the person I am. I'm glad I paid attention, because I ended up with a husband who is funny, kind, supportive, and adoring."

We romance readers can separate ridiculous from reality, and fact from fiction. We don't expect all men to be billionaire tycoon dukes who are also Navy SEAL spies and fluent in sixty-nine languages. Not a single one of those things guarantees happiness, or a happily-ever-after.

But because of what we've learned about healthy, admirable relationships, we *do* expect men to be partners in our lives, to listen, care, pay attention, and treat us as if we are valuable and special. That is what helps foster happiness. No billions, yachts, or tactical weapons experience necessary.

Reader Caroline learned that lesson from her own romance-reading: "Romance novels in general taught me that it isn't about the bling, but the substance behind the bling that makes it last. Always the heroine and hero, at some level, just want to be with one another by the end of the book. I have rarely read a book where the heroine goes, 'Well…He's a billionaire-playboy-oil-baron-secret-Earl-Sheik with a whole barnful of horses, six palatial mansions, and a bunch of jets; I guess I'll be happy with him. Oh yeah, and he's got a magic wang.' It's always a little deeper than that. The person usually comes to the surface. The need for the person outweighs the trappings, and there is never a second guess.

"There were a few books I read that taught me love is not easy. It takes work. Just because someone gets you all hot in the pants doesn't mean it's going to be a cakewalk down the aisle. You sometimes have to compromise, sometimes examine yourself first, and talk to one another, not just humpity-hump until you say the L-word and have the Twue Lurve ending. Sometimes shit gets in the way and you have to deal."

> We romance readers can separate ridiculous from reality, and fact from fiction. We don't expect all men to be billionaire tycoon dukes who are also Navy SEAL spies and fluent in sixty-nine languages.

Editor Angela James loves J. D. Robb's In Death series because of its portrayal of the courtship of marriage: "One of the things I love about that series is the progression of the romance, from courtship to lovers to marriage, where you see the relationship grow and build. And Ms. Robb does a fantastic job of showing the give and take of marriage, and being partners and equals. I think this makes an even bigger impression on me than many romance novels because I'm at a different stage in my life. I'm not looking for love or falling in love, but I'm in love with someone I know is 'it.' And since maintaining the relationship in a marriage has its own unique challenges, it's nice to see an author tackling those and not creating a world where the marriage is perfect, without flaws, and doesn't face adversity."

> "Nothing gives me greater pleasure in my entertainment than reading about people who, with real (as opposed to contrived) problems, overcome them in a sane, healthy, and productive way that sets them up for life."
>
> —ROBYN CARR

Robyn Carr says she envies her characters sometimes: "The unvarnished truth is—I often wish I was as smart as my characters. I wish that, in real life, I could delete and rewrite the things I say, adjust the things I do and make them more intelligent, control the unexpected events in my life. I think reading and writing romances is very good practice for living within relationships—it helps us separate the wheat from the chaff. We know what not to do (in each individual opinion) and we get a good view of things that might actually work. I really appreciate it when characters in trouble get help; I cheer characters who know they're fallible and want to overcome their weaknesses or faults. My heart races with pleasure when they reach a mutual understanding that gives them a chance at happiness.

"Nothing gives me greater pleasure in my entertainment than reading about people who, with real (as opposed to contrived) problems, overcome them in a sane, healthy, and productive way that sets them up for life."

The fantasy of seeing a painful and horrific situation resolve toward hope and happiness is another reason why romance readers are such avid and enduring fans of the genre. Each novel is a safe emotional space to examine awkward and potentially tricky emotions and see that each experience, and each character, can achieve happiness—a happiness well worth achieving.

ROMANCE AND COURTSHIP IN THREE EASY STEPS

It might seem that a mammoth serving of romance novels comes equipped with unending relationship wisdom—and it does, but not because one has read fourteen million novels. Whether one has read a handful or has a book in each hand every day of the year, the basic lessons on relationships and unending courtships are pretty simple to spot.

1. DON'T TAKE PEOPLE FOR GRANTED

Whether it's your parents, your partner, or your favorite train conductor, the people in your life won't always be there. It's reassuring to think so, that the people who make your life warm and whole will always be with you, but the truth is, life is far too uncertain to make that kind of guarantee—so you shouldn't take the people in your life for granted. Ever.

You never know when a tycoon may sweep you onto his yacht, or when a last will and testament of an aunt you didn't know you had might indicate you stand to inherit a huge palatial property in the Canary Islands—provided you marry a prince and live in that palatial property with your worst enemy and a dog named Doof. Kidnappings, ghost possessions, vampire infestations, getting fired, opening a bake shop and finding out the recipes are all witchcraft, one-night stands in bathrooms at an ex-girlfriend's wedding…look, these things happen. Conflict happens.

> Not only should you be prepared for conflict, but you should know that each day brings the chance for more of it-billionaires are not much for advanced warning when they arrive on their yachts with plans for blackmail.

Not only should you be prepared for conflict, but you

should know that each day brings the chance for more of it—billionaires are not much for advanced warning when they arrive on their yachts with plans for blackmail. With the chance for changes ahoy each day, it's important that you stop yourself every now and again from presuming that every morning will be like the one before.

Acknowledge the people you like. Merely going through the motions of your routine does nothing to communicate to others how you think of them. So thank people for being spiffy, and find ways to express that you're glad someone is in your life, whether it's the bus driver who always says good morning with a smile, or the person who makes the coffee every single evening and sets the timer so that when the alarm goes off, it's ready.

Demonstrating love and affection for a significant other in a romance is part of courtship, particularly the part that might involve sex. But you most commonly see characters realizing that they're taking someone they care about for granted in plots that involve family as part of the cast of characters—it is very easy to take your family for granted, after all—or in stories where the hero and heroine have been friends for a very, very long time, and suddenly find themselves at a point of massive change or departure—he's leaving, she's sick of being alone, whatever.

Being in the habit of saying "Thank you," of making sure that people receive attention so they know you value them, of not presuming that people will always be there—this is a good habit, regardless of whether you're in a relationship or still hoping to find a person who makes you happy in your pants and your brain.

Consider this: **The Be Polite Rule: Don't be a douche-bag**. Make sure the people who are important to you receive attention for being awesome. There's plenty of crapful behavior on the part of random douchebags in a given day—make sure to give virtual and actual high-fives to those who rock and rock hard.

2. SAY IT NOW

One of the most enduring lessons I learned about love was not from a romance novel, but from a romance author. A long time ago, I wanted to write romance—before I realized my writing strength may not be in writing fiction. When I first started meeting romance authors and going to romance conferences back in 2002, I volunteered to pick up authors at the airport before the New Jersey Romance Writer's convention, and ended up driving bestselling author Teresa Medeiros to the hotel from the airport. She is, if you've never met her, among the nicest people you'll ever meet, and her books are good too—a total bonus.

Teresa had to call her husband to let him know she arrived safely, so there we were, flying down the New Jersey Turnpike, me, Teresa, and bestselling author (and later RWA President) Gayle Wilson. Teresa made her call, and ended the call by saying, "I love you."

Now, this may not seem like a big deal, but at the time, I was newly married, a little shy (okay, a lot shy), and would not have been able to tell my husband on the phone that I loved him in front of two strangers. I don't think Gayle Wilson cared in the least but I, personally, was *so* impressed.

I should mention that I'd misplaced the directions to the hotel and we had to call from the car to get them from the hotel—and I did almost tell the hotel front desk clerk that I loved her, if only because she saved me from more embarrassment.

But I continued to think about Medeiros and her phone call, and to this day, I don't hang up the phone with my husband without telling him I love him, even when I know he can't say it back to me.

Say it now. Don't save it. Right now is the most important moment to tell someone you value them and think they are made of awesome with sauce.

Consider this: **The Medeiros Rule: Never miss an opportunity to tell someone or communicate to someone that they are loved.**

3. IT'S NOT ALL ABOUT YOU

If there is one lesson inherent in romance novels that is important for every person, regardless of gender, to internalize and believe to the utmost, it is the idea that you are valuable, you are important, and your happiness is important. As reader Liz says in a discussion of hero and heroine traits, "You are valuable. You are important. We will never forget that about each other. That's romance, to me."

Yet with all these chapters that examine how romance has

helped readers identify what they want in a relationship, and all the plots that rest on establishing and knowing one's own worth, I have some important words about your happily-ever-after: it's not all about you.

No, really, it's not all about you. Consider Liz's words, which I think of as T**he Liz Rule: "You are valuable. You are important. We will never forget that about each other." Part of being in a relationship that is solid and mature is making sure the other person knows they are valuable in your eyes.** The most important relationship you might have is indeed with yourself, but all that self-love can get lonely and unsatisfying if you don't also know how to communicate to someone else how valuable they are to you.

HEALING THROUGH BOOKS
BY ANONYMOUS

For some, romance novels are not only a lifeline and escape, they are a guideline, proof somehow that a happy ending is possible. The following is a painful, somewhat graphic, and very honest person's account of how romance novels have been a meaningful part of her life. She wrote this as part of a personal recovery exercise, but gave me permission to share it so long as I protected her identity.

> When I was ten years old, eleven, twelve, I needed to get away. I so desperately needed it, every time my mom's boyfriend would come into my room and rape

me, because I couldn't stand to be there and face what was going on. It was too much for me, to be in this world. So, I found some place else I could be, some place I was safe and okay. Some place I was loved and cared about. Some place no one would hurt me, and where good would always, always triumph over evil. And I found it in the pages of books.

I remember the first time I actually jumped into a book. It was a children's mystery book, about a group of friends who wanted to find out what was in the dark, old house on their street, where they'd seen shadows. And I remember reading it, and feeling *in* the house, exploring it with them. It was so real to me; I could smell the mold and feel the spiderwebs clinging to my arms as I walked through the dark hallway. I could feel the fear of the "ghost" or whatever was in there (it was a parrot, haha), the excitement of a new discovery. I was instantly transported to another world, a world where everything was okay, and I didn't have to be afraid.

Through that hardest time of my life, I read. I read day and night. I read whenever I could get my hands on a book, because I didn't want to be in the real world. I hated the real world. I needed to get away. And I did. Many times, when he would get to me at night, I found myself thinking about the stories I'd read, about the worlds I'd visited, and it kept me from hurting so much at that moment. It didn't work every time, but whenever it did, it was relief from all the pain.

For the first few years after the abuse, I think I was in shock, because I didn't process what happened. It was like a faded distant memory, the abuse. I didn't think about it at all. Because, really, I didn't have time to think. Because I read. All the time. One book after another. I was never without a book. I remember going to school and reading through classes, reading in the car on my way home, at the lunch—and dinner—table, waking up early on a weekend to read and staying up late to read. It was all books, books, and books (with the eventual TV show!). And I went through this period of my life so smoothly, thanks to God and thanks to books, because, honestly, I don't know what would have happened to me if I'd had to deal with the aftermath of abuse at thirteen, fourteen, fifteen.

When I was fifteen, it finally dawned on me about the abuse. And not only did I keep reading (a lot!), I started writing. I knew when I was eleven that I wanted to be an author when I grew up, because I loved telling stories, because they took me away from the world, and, most importantly, because I wanted to give other people that needed it a safe place to go. I wrote short stories, created my own characters, my own worlds. I kept reading too. I read and I read and I read through the following years. The summer of when I was seventeen, I read seventeen books in a month. It could have been a miserable summer; instead, it was fun and free. I wasn't alone, ever, because I had characters to keep me company. I wasn't sad, because the books made me laugh. I wasn't bored, because, hello? Books! It was one of the greatest summers of my life.

In my late teens, I was going through a huge turmoil. I was extremely confused because I knew exactly what had happened to me, I remembered all of it, and I didn't know how that affected me. I kept seeing at abuse groups how messed up people were, and I didn't want to be like that. I kept seeing how easy it was to give in and feel sorry for yourself, and I didn't want to be like that. So I read. And when I read, I found characters who'd gone through some of the same things I had. Characters who had become strong, independent, healed women, despite what had happened to them. And I looked up to those women. That's what I wanted to be like, not a great big mess. I wanted to be okay! And, in books, I found a way to do that. Little steps, but these fictional characters helped me follow the right path.

Later things got even more complicated. I made a lot of bad decisions. I did some really stupid things. I started having my bipolar crisis, which left me in a state where I couldn't control myself. I felt the world was falling apart, and there was just no way to stop it. And I wanted out. I wanted out of here ASAP. But there were books. And not only did books take me away when I really needed to get out of here—I could do it temporarily instead of permanently—but they gave me a reason to live. I mean, how could I possibly kill myself when there were so many books for me to read? So many characters to discover? So many worlds to see? I couldn't. And I lived, one day after the other.

I can't count the times I've wanted to die, really wanted to die, and instead, I grabbed a book and flipped through the pages, looking for comfort, for care and understanding. Crying, so many times I sat crying, because those words on the page were the only understanding I'd ever gotten, because they were the only company I had, the only "friends" who didn't look at me superficially and neglected to see my pain. I'd sit there, biting my lip so hard it bled, reading the same pages over and over and over, because there was a happy ending—and if *she* could have a happy ending, she who was so hurt by her family, by that guy, by that serial killer, by life itself—then so could I. If a "hero" looked at her and saw beyond her scars, if he didn't care that she was sexually abused, that she was messed up, there could be a guy like that for me, couldn't there? I wouldn't want to miss that. So I lived to find out. And I still do.

When I say books saved me, I'm not exaggerating. If it weren't for books—that gave me comfort, friendship, understanding, and hope—I don't think I would have survived through everything I did. They make it all seem worthy, you know? It's like, no matter what you go through in your life, how hard it is, how messed up, there's always hope, there's always someone, there's always a happy ending. And, believing that makes me go on.

I wonder if authors know how much their words matter, how much they can truly change someone's life. In the last year, I've started reading authors' blogs, and I see them struggling to get the words on the page, sometimes exhausted, sometimes annoyed, sometimes over it. I know they ask themselves, sometimes, whether it's worth it, to give everything of themselves, for sometimes shitty pay and bad reviews (even when their books are great!). I wish I could tell them all that there's someone out there, someone who needs to get away from the world, someone who's hurting more than they can handle, maybe someone who is thinking about killing themselves and looking for a reason not to, who is going to pick up their book tonight and let it be their safe haven. Who will forget the pain for a while, and just go to another world. They're going to meet new people. They get to not be themselves for a while, and sometimes, that's what they need the most. Maybe they'll find a reason to live. Sometimes, I want to write a note to every author I've read during my hardest times. A single sentence: "Thank you for saving my life."

"Without books, I wouldn't be here today. I wouldn't be as healed...With books you're never alone. Books are friends."—ANONYMOUS, A READER

Many years later, I still want to be an author. I want, more than anything, to give someone a safe place to go, give them freedom, friends, love, and understanding. I want to save lives. So to answer your question, what helped me the most in the process of healing were books. Stories. Fictional stories with great characters and happy endings. Without books, I wouldn't be here today. I wouldn't be as healed. And I am. I've come such a long way. With books you're never alone. Books are friends.

The Final Chapter:
The Happy Ending Starts...Now

.... ♥ ....

If you're the type of person who skips to the end of a book, you're in luck. I'm going to summarize everything about this book in one easy chapter. Here you go, the low-fat, high-fiber summary of everything you need to know about romance as found in the awesome romance section of your local bookstore.

Romance is how we treat each other, and how we treat ourselves.

Romance is a habit, much like Vince Lombardi said of winning. It is not presuming that the people who love you know that you love them, nor assuming that they will always be around you. Romance is demonstrating in as many ways as possible, through actions, words, and intentions, that the people you love are important, valuable, and necessary.

Romance is also in how you treat yourself: with compassion, kindness, respect, and understanding. It is important to know what you want, and to ask for it, because you are valuable and important as well.

LIFE LESSONS HIDDEN IN ROMANCE NOVELS

AMNESIAC TWINS	Truthfulness and self-identification are very important. Otherwise, you might go out to find yourself, and return to find you're already there. That would be confusing.
COWBOY HEROES	A quiet, loner dude who wears well-fitting Wranglers and possibly chaps without irony or embarrassment can be a fine, fine specimen of manhood, particularly if his job is to care for a few hundred thousand animals. Care-giving in the harshest of elements speaks volumes.
BIG MISUNDER-STANDINGS	Oh, come on now. This is obvious. What do you mean you don't know what I'm thinking? I'm not telling you, so you have to figure it out on your own.
DUKES, DUCHESSES, EARLS, COUNTESSES, AND ALL THE OTHER TITLES	The real riches in life aren't physical things or letters before or after your names. They are found in the person standing next to you, cracking jokes in a receiving line that's two miles and six hours long.
CROSS DRESSING	Look, if you are a twenty-four-year-old woman who can fit in a twelve-year-old boy's clothing, more power to you. You don't need a romance novel. But you might want to eat a sandwich or two.
TIME TRAVEL	No matter where you go, there you are. Ha. Kidding. The life lesson hidden in time-travel romance is that the first thing you will miss when you find yourself a few dozen years forward or back is your toothbrush.

Romance is in the small moments and the motivation behind a quiet gift or action. Demonstrating your affection does not necessarily mean chartering a yacht to sail around the world. A big chocolaty, flowery gesture of Valentine cliché does not automatically equal romance. But filling her gas tank when you notice it's empty, or cooking his favorite meal after a really crappy day at work—all those little moments combine to portray a clear affection. The gesture is not the romance; the motivation for the gesture is.

ROMANCE IS NOT ALL ABOUT YOU

As I wrote in an article for *Tango* magazine, romance is not about getting some; it's about giving some. Romance does require that you understand your own needs and wants, but it's equally important to notice and acknowledge the desires and needs of the person you're with—or the person you want to be with. Romance is valuing the other person's happiness as much as you value your own.

ROMANCE MEANS ROUTINE CARE AND MAINTENANCE

You can't drive cross-country without gas in the tank, and you can't have a happily-ever-after without simple care and feeding of your relationship. You can't take people for granted, and you can't ignore those small moments of appreciation and acknowlededgement. Romance can be as simple as saying "Please" and

"Thank you." For example: Please know that your being here makes me happy. Thank you for making me smile.

ROMANCE MEANS LOVING SOMEONE FOR WHO THEY ARE, RIGHT NOW

Romance is truthful—in the sense that you don't lie your pants off, and you don't pretend to be someone you are not. You should be able to reveal your true self to the person who loves you, and they'll love you exactly as you are. Romance is knowing that you are loved without any requests or demands for change. To quote Shakespeare (Oh, come on, I had to do it once): "Love is not love that alters when it alteration finds, nor bends with the remover to remove. It is an ever-fixed mark that looks on tempests and is never shaken."

ROMANCE MEANS BELIEVING YOU ARE WORTHY OF A HAPPY ENDING—AND WANTING TO GIVE ONE TO SOMEONE ELSE

Everyone deserves happiness, and the knowledge that they are loved and awesome just the way they are. The trick to a happily-ever-after is knowing that the ever-after starts now. Right now. No, really.

May we all be happy, may we all feel the joy of romance, and may we all live happily ever after.

"When our heroines walk away from lying, cheating, abusive relationships, our readers stand up and cheer! When our heroes fail to fall for mean, selfish, manipulative women, our readers applaud! Men and women in real life and in romance novels find themselves trapped in unhealthy, destructive relationships all the time, and when they choose to believe they deserve love, respect, and healthy, enduring relationships, when they reclaim their lives and demand only excellent treatment and a love they can fully trust, life is good."

—ROBYN CARR

XO

Sources

Bahls, Patrick. "DocTurtle Returns to Finish *Lord of Scoundrels*." http://www.smartbitchestrashybooks.com/index.php/weblog/comments/docturtle-returns-to-finish-lord-of-scoundrels/, retrieved 12 November 2010.

Campbell, Anna. Personal interview, 12 October 2010.

Chase, Loretta. Personal interview, 12 November 2010.

Crusie, Jennifer. Personal interview, 15 October 2010.

Donnelly, Denise A., quoted in "When Sex Leaves the Marriage." *New York Times*, 3 June 2009. http://well.blogs.nytimes.com/2009/06/03/when-sex-leaves-the-marriage, retrieved 7 December 2010.

Finlay, Janet, Director of Market Research, Harlequin Enterprises Ltd. Personal interview, 16 November 2010.

Hayes, Donna. Speech at Spring Fling YWCA-NY, New York, New York, 24 June 2010.

James, Eloisa. Personal interview, 13 October 2010.

MacLean, Sarah. Personal interview, 12 November 2010.

Medeiros, Teresa. "A Romantic Hero Wouldn't Do That." http://articles.cnn.com/2010-05-31/living/tiger.jesse.romance.heroes_1_romance-hero-romance-writers-true-love?_s=PM:LIVING, retrieved 6 March 2011.

Roberts, Nora. Personal interview, 14 October 2010.

RWA Statistics on Romance Readership. http://www.rwa.org/cs/readership_stats, retrieved 7 June 2011.

Schoenthaler, Robin. "Will he hold your purse?" http://www.boston.com/bostonglobe/magazine/articles/2009/10/04/will_he_hold_your_purse/, retrieved 27 November 2010.

Shopping List

················ ♥ ················

The following titles are quoted in this book and appear here in list form, should the excerpts make you want to read more—which they probably do.

☐ *Bet Me* by Jennifer Crusie (St. Martin's, 2004)

☐ *Caressed by Ice* by Nalini Singh (Penguin/Berkley, 2007)

☐ *Dark Needs at Night's Edge* by Kresley Cole (Pocket, 2008)

☐ *Devil in Winter* by Lisa Kleypas (Avon, 2006)

☐ *The Duke and I* by Julia Quinn (Avon, 2000)

☐ *Heaven and Earth* by Nora Roberts (Penguin/Berkley Jove, 2001)

☐ *Instant Attraction* by Jill Shalvis (Kensington, 2009)

☐ *Just One of the Guys* by Kristan Higgins (HQN, 2008)

☐ *Last Night's Scandal* by Loretta Chase (Avon, 2010)

☐ *Lord of Scoundrels* by Loretta Chase (Avon, 1995)

- ☐ *Rising Tides* by Nora Roberts (Penguin, 1998)
- ☐ *Unveiled* by Courtney Milan (Harlequin, 2010)

About the Author

Sarah Wendell, more commonly known as Smart Bitch Sarah, is cofounder and current mastermind of *Smart Bitches, Trashy Books*, one of the most popular review blogs devoted to the romance genre. She is also coauthor of the book *Beyond Heaving Bosoms: The Smart Bitches' Guide to Romance Novels*. Sarah is a frequent speaker at national and regional conferences on subjects as diverse as romance cover art, digital reading, and social media promotion and marketing. A former Pittsburgher, Sarah resides in northern New Jersey. Sarah can be found online at smartbitchestrashybooks.com, or at SBSarah.com, or via Twitter at @smartbitches.

Sarah also dreads writing these types of bios, so she asked Twitter for suggestions:

"Sarah leads the mantitty masterclass."—@tenthmuse
Sarah is not sure how to describe that one in the course catalog.

"Go for brevity: 'Smart Bitch Sarah is teh awesumest.'"
—@jennybullough
Unfortunately, Sarah is unsure if she can say that with a straight face.

"Sarah always Helps a Bitch Out."—@cjewel
Sarah tries, and is flattered by the compliment.

"As Inventor of HABO, SW helps readers find books hovering at the edge of their consciousness, making the world a better place."
—@susanmpls
Sarah believes that the more crazysauce an old romance plot is, the more we all have to reread it!

"Sarah writes the best contest disclaimers ever, and is a supporter of libraries."—@ksattler
Sarah loves libraries! Void where prohibited!

"Don't forget to mention your ninja training."—@jesidres
Yes, yes, of course! Sarah is a ninja. OF LOVE.